Modern Critical Interpretations

Robert Penn Warren's
All the King's Men

Modern Critical Interpretations

These and other titles in preparation

Robert Penn Warren's
All the King's Men

Edited and with an introduction by

Harold Bloom
Sterling Professor of the Humanities
Yale University

Chelsea House Publishers ◊ *1987*
NEW YORK ◊ NEW HAVEN ◊ PHILADELPHIA

© 1987 by Chelsea House Publishers,
a division of Chelsea House Educational Communications, Inc.,
  95 Madison Avenue, New York, NY 10016
  345 Whitney Avenue, New Haven, CT 06511
  5014 West Chester Pike, Edgemont, PA 19028

Introduction © 1987 by Harold Bloom

Printed and bound in the United States of America

10 9 8 7 6 5 4 3 2 1

∞ The paper used in this publication meets the minimum
requirements of the American National Standard for
Permanence of Paper for Printed Library Materials,
Z39.48–1984.

Library of Congress Cataloging-in-Publication Data
Robert Penn Warren's All the king's men.
  (Modern critical interpretations)
  Bibliography: p.
  Includes index.
  Summary: A collection of critical essays on Warren's
novel "All the King's Men" arranged in chronological
order of publication.
  1. Warren, Robert Penn, 1905–   . All the king's
men. [1. Warren, Robert Penn, 1905–   . All the
king's men.   2. American literature—History and
criticism]   I. Bloom, Harold.   II. Series.
PS3545.A748A7958 1987   813'.52   87-5209
ISBN 1–55546–063–1 (alk. paper)

Contents

Editor's Note

This volume brings together what I judge to be a representative selection of the most useful criticism available of Robert Penn Warren's novel *All the King's Men,* arranged in the chronological order of the critical essays' first publication. I thank Neil Arditi for his aid in helping me to edit this book.

My introduction centers upon the problematical relationship between Willie Stark, the novel's hero-villain, and the narrator, Jack Burden. The chronological sequence of criticism begins with Charles Kaplan's comparison of Burden and Melville's Ishmael in *Moby-Dick.* Jonathan Baumbach views Burden as a partly fulfilled spiritual voyager, while Arthur Mizener gives us a Burden about equally divided between Stark's realism and Adam Stanton's idealism.

In reading *All the King's Men* as a philosophical novel, Allen Shepherd presents Warren as something of a pragmatist, in the mode of William James. Murray Krieger, playing upon Jack Burden's name, achieves an analytical sense of the book as the burden of Burden's self-education.

From the perspective of southern American history, Richard Gray reads the novel as a dialectical interpretation between past and present. Emphasis changes to narrative structure in Simone Vauthier's inquiry, which traces the evanescence of the "you" to whom Jack Burden's story is told.

Richard G. Law, in an exegesis of the nature of truth in Warren's novel, finds the moral center in Burden's final awareness that while experiential contradictions qualify every truth, we must not yield to mere subjectivism in our quest for realities. In this book's final essay, Richard H. King sharply studies what he calls a transition from politics to psychology in Warren's best novel, a transition that he judges to be a decline from profound political responsibility to a private quest for identity. Whether King is too severe in lamenting Burden's (and Warren's) choice of an individual or Romantic secular salvation is not clear to me, but his argument is another tribute to the ongoing relevance of *All the King's Men*.

Introduction

Warren's first book was *John Brown: The Making of a Martyr* (1929). I have just read it, for the first time, and discovered, without surprise, that it made me very unhappy. The book purports to be history, but is southern fiction of Allen Tate's ideology and portrays Brown as a murderous nihilist, fit hero for Ralph Waldo Emerson. Indeed I find it difficult to decide, after suffering the book, whether the young Warren loathed Brown or Emerson more. Evidently, both Brown and his intellectual supporter seemed, to Warren, instances of an emptiness making ruthless and passionate attempts to prove itself a fullness. But *John Brown,* if read as a first fiction, does presage the Warren of *Night Rider* (1939), his first published novel, which I have just reread with great pleasure.

Night Rider is an exciting and remorseless narrative, wholly characteristic of what were to be Warren's prime virtues as a novelist: good story-telling and intensely dramatic unfolding of the moral character of his doom-eager men and women. Mr. Munn, upon whom *Night Rider* centers, is as splendidly unsympathetic as the true Warren heroes continued to be: Jerry Calhoun and Slim Sarrett in *At Heaven's Gate* (1943), Jack Burden and Willie Stark in *All the King's Men* (1946), Jeremiah Beaumont and Cassius Fort in *World Enough and Time* (1950). When Warren's crucial personages turned more amiable, starting with poor Amantha Starr in *Band of Angels* (1955), the books alas turned much less interesting. This unfortunate phenomenon culminated in Warren's last novel (so far), *A Place to Come To* (1977), which Warren himself ranks with *All the King's Men* and *World Enough and Time.* I wish I could agree, but rereading *A Place to Come To* confirms an earlier impression that Warren likes his hero,

Jed Tewksbury, rather too much. Without some real moral distaste to goad him, Warren tends to lose his narrative drive. I find myself wishing that Tewksbury had in him a touch of what might be called Original John Brown.

Warren's true precursor, as a novelist, was not Faulkner but Conrad, the dominant influence upon so many of the significant American novelists of Warren's generation. In one of his best critical essays, written in 1951 on Conrad's *Nostromo,* Warren gave an unknowing clue as to why all his own best work, as a novelist, already was over:

> There is another discrepancy, or apparent discrepancy, that we must confront in any serious consideration of Conrad—that between his professions of skepticism and his professions of faith. . . .
>
> Cold unconcern, an "attitude of perfect indifference" is, as he says in the letter to Galsworthy, "the part of creative power." But this is the same Conrad who speaks of Fidelity and the human communion, and who makes Kurtz cry out in the last horror and Heyst come to his vision of meaning in life. And this is the same Conrad who makes Marlow of "Heart of Darkness" say that what redeems is the "idea only.". . .
>
> It is not some, but all, men who must serve the "idea." The lowest and the most vile creature must, in some way, idealize his existence in order to exist, and must find sanctions outside himself.

Warren calls this a reading of Conrad's dual temperament, skepticism struggling with a last-ditch idealism, and remarks, much in T. S. Eliot's spirit:

> We must sometimes force ourselves to remember that the act of creation is not simply a projection of temperament, but a criticism and a purging of temperament.

This New Critical shibboleth becomes wholly Eliotic if we substitute the word "personality" for the word "temperament." As an analysis of Conrad's dramatism in his best novels, and in *Nostromo* in particular, this has distinction, but Warren is not Conrad, and like his poetic and critical precursor, Eliot, Warren creates by projecting temperament, not by purging it. There is no "cold unconcern," no "attitude of perfect indifference," no escape from personality in Eliot, and even more nakedly Warren's novels and poems continually reveal his passions, prejudices, convictions. Conrad is majestically enigmatic, beyond ideology; Warren, like Eliot, is an ideologue, and his temperament is far more ferocious than Eliot's.

What Warren accurately praises in Conrad is not to be found in Warren's own novels, with the single exception of *All the King's Men,* which does balance skepticism against belief just adroitly enough to ward off Warren's moralism. *World Enough and Time,* Warren's last stand as a major novelist, is an exuberant work marred finally by the author's singular fury at his own creatures. As a person who forgives himself nothing, Warren abandons the Conradian skepticism and proceeds to forgive his hero and heroine nothing. Rereading *World Enough and Time,* I wince repeatedly at what the novelist inflicts upon Jeremiah Beaumont and Rachel Jordan. Warren, rather like the Gnostics' parody of Jehovah, punishes *his* Adam and Eve by denying them honorable or romantic deaths. Their joint suicide drug turns into an emetic, and every kind of degradation subsequently is heaped upon them. Warren, a superb ironist, nevertheless so loves the world that he will forgive it nothing, a stance more pragmatically available to a poet than to a novelist.

II

I first read *All the King's Men* as a Cornell undergraduate in the late 1940s, under the tutelage of a great teacher, William M. Sale, who remarked of the book that it had nearly every possible flaw, but that it was also unmistakably part of the permanent tradition or canon of the American novel. Sale's canonical judgment, uttered only two or three years after the novel's first publication (1946) has been confirmed. Rereading the book now, nearly forty years after first studying it, I marvel at its triumph over the author's restless temperament. Too passionate a moralist, perhaps too great a visionary, to cultivate the patience of a novelist, Warren instead became a major poet, probably our finest since the death of Wallace Stevens. *All the King's Men* is likely to be his principal legacy after the extraordinary poetry he has written in the two decades since 1966.

Remembering *All the King's Men,* I had thought of it as Willie Stark's story; rereading it, I see that it is far more Jack Burden's than it is Stark's. Warren is ambivalent enough towards Stark; in regard to Burden, "ambivalence" seems almost too weak a term for Warren's stance. The author nearly identifies himself with his narrator, yet that identification is dialectical in the mode of what Freud called "negation." Burden is Warren's burden: a cognitive return of the repressed while the affective aspect of repression continues. The mind of Robert Penn Warren at meridian is introjected as Jack Burden, while the passional life of Warren, domain of the drives, is projected and so spit out as Burden, morally rejected by his creator, in a way that Willie Stark is not, if only because Stark is stark—strong and active—where Burden is weak and passive, a burden to himself and to others.

Yet he remains, to me, Warren's most interesting fictive person, perhaps because he is and is not Warren, the portrait of the artist as a failed (momentarily) youngish man. One of the hidden splendors, tawdry yet fascinating, of the novel is Burden's failed first marriage (as it will prove to be, since at the end, he does marry Anne Stanton). The truth of the first marriage emerges with a fine clarity in the famous sentence that ends Burden's account of it: "Good-bye, Lois, and I forgive you for everything I did to you." The bitterness is only towards the self, for only the self existed. When he cannot bring the past alive into the present, then Burden becomes a pure solipsist, aware neither of neighbors nor of the sun.

It is the peculiar strength of Willie Stark that he breaks through Burden's defenses sufficiently so that the novel's narrator becomes at most an imperfect solipsist, brilliantly capable of telling an intensely dramatic story. *All the King's Men*'s prime literary virtue is the wonderfully old-fashioned one of being compulsively readable. That this is wholly due to Willie Stark is unquestionable. He is one of the last authentic hero-villains of the high Jacobean mode, worthy of a twentieth-century John Webster, or of Faulkner, or even of Conrad. Burden's relation to Stark is not that of Conrad's Marlow to Kurtz in *Heart of Darkness,* or of Faulkner's Quentin to Sutpen in *Absalom, Absalom!,* but rather is that of Warren himself to the historical figure of the Kingfish, Huey Long of Louisiana. This necessarily has caused some confusions in the critical apprehension of *All the King's Men.* Burden's barely repressed love for Stark, essentially filial in nature, does not represent Warren's hidden fondness for the most persuasive of our country's native Fascists, our Franco or Mussolini, as it were. Rather, Stark's fascination for Warren is dramatic, and aesthetic, even as it is for us as Warren's readers.

The movement from the factual, historical Huey Long to the fictive Willie Stark is epitomized by the difference between Long's "I know the hearts of the people because I have not colored my own" and Stark's "My study is the heart of the people." Willie is pithier than Huey, and even more persuasive. He is the answer to a universal Oedipus complex, an answer conveyed most poignantly in the novel's central moment, the final meeting between Jack Burden and his crucial father-substitute, Willie Stark, dying but still the Boss:

> He lifted the forefinger and the next finger of his right hand, which lay prone on the sheet, in an incipient salute, then let them drop. The strength of the muscles which held his mouth twisted gave out, too, and the grin slid off his face and the weight of flesh sagged back.
>
> I stood up close to the bed and looked down at him, and tried to think of something to say. But my brain felt as juiceless as an old sponge left out in the sun a long time.
>
> Then he said, in something a little better than a whisper, "I wanted to see you, Jack."
>
> "I wanted to see you, too, Boss."
>
> For a minute he didn't speak, but his eyes looked up at me, with the light still flickering in them. Then he spoke: "Why did he do it to me?"
>
> "Oh, God damn it," I burst out, very loud, "I don't know."
>
> The nurse looked warningly at me.
>
> "I never did anything to him," he said.
>
> "No, you never did."
>
> He was silent again, and the flicker went down in his eyes. Then, "He was all right. The Doc."
>
> I nodded.
>
> I waited, but it began to seem that he wasn't going to say any more. His eyes were on the ceiling and I could scarcely tell that he was breathing. Finally, the eyes turned toward me again, very slowly, and I almost thought that I could hear the tiny painful creak of the balls in their sockets. But the light flickered up again. He said, "It might have been all different, Jack."
>
> I nodded again.
>
> He roused himself more. He even seemed to be straining to lift his head from the pillow. "You got to believe that," he said hoarsely.

The nurse stepped forward and looked significantly at me.

"Yes," I said to the man on the bed.

"You got to," he said again. "You got to believe that."

"All right."

He looked at me, and for a moment it was the old strong, probing, demanding glance. But when the words came this time, they were very weak. "And it might even been different yet," he whispered. "If it hadn't happened, it might—have been different—even yet."

He barely got the last words out, he was so weak.

The nurse was making signals to me.

I reached down and took the hand on the sheet. It felt like a piece of jelly.

"So long, Boss," I said. "I'll be seeing you."

He didn't answer, and I wasn't even sure that there was recognition in the eyes now. I turned away and went out.

It is the father as man-of-action saying farewell to his true son as intellectual or spiritual discerner, and trying, somewhat heroically, to give a final blessing by way of expiation. For Willie Stark has been a castrating father, and in ways that transcended his taking Anne Stanton away from Jack Burden. "It might—have been different—even yet" is more than a political reference or ruined social prophecy. As a reference to the buried relationship between Stark and Burden, it implies a belated recognition of the burden of a better fatherhood, and better filial vision, than either figure has known before. That seems the profoundest meaning of Burden's final rumination that concludes the novel:

> We shall come back, no doubt, to walk down the Row and watch young people on the tennis courts by the clump of mimosas and walk down the beach by the bay, where the diving floats lift gently in the sun, and on out to the pine grove, where the needles thick on the ground will deaden the footfall so that we shall move among trees as soundlessly as smoke. But that will be a long time from now, and soon now we shall go out of the house and go into the convulsion of the world, out of history into history and the awful responsibility of Time.

To go out of history into history is to take up Time's awful responsibility of the agon between fathers and sons, never confronted by Stark and Burden, who evaded their mutual recognition until it was too late.

Jack Burden: Modern Ishmael

Charles Kaplan

The story is told in the first person by a young man who has something of importance to tell us about his past experiences. In order to communicate the meaning of those experiences, he has to make us relive them with him. Consequently, he does not flatly and inartistically give away the "ending," instead, he recreates his adventures retrospectively, both as a means of defining to himself the nature of what has happened to him and as a means of dramatically involving the passive reader. As he tells the narrative, he finds himself faced with the usual kinds of technical difficulties which writers of fiction must resolve: the vantage-point of the narrator, the relevant incidents, the sequence of those incidents, the problems of foreshortening and focusing, the symbols, the language and the tone, and so on. The young man adopts a narrative strategy designed to evoke the desired effect in his readers.

Briefly summarized, his story revolves about a crisis in his life, during which time he comes under the influence of an almost superhumanly powerful personality in a position of unchallengeable authority. As the narrator tells the story, he himself seems to become a secondary participant or even fade from the picture, and the strong authoritarian individual grows until he dominates the scene completely. This man, perfectly at home in his world, expresses his attitude toward it by towering contemptuously above his fellow-creatures. For him, understanding has led not to humility but to

From *College English* 22, no. 1 (October 1960). © 1960 by the National Council of Teachers of English.

9

arrogance. His behavior reveals assumptions concerning his own infallibility, as he begins to play God and to impose his own ideas about the world on intractable nature. The consequence of such colossal pride is downfall and death. But the young man, watching and reporting this career, undergoes a significant change: as the stronger figure loses contact with humanity, eventually to die, the narrator moves in a reverse pattern, eventually to be reintegrated, to rejoin the world of human beings from which he had originally felt himself alienated. Or, to use a more precise figure of speech which the narrator himself supplies, he is "reborn."

The faceless account given above will naturally suggest to many readers the plan of *Moby-Dick*. But, in the words of W. H. Auden, "Most American books might well start like *Moby-Dick*. 'Call me Ishmael.' . . . Most American novels are parables, their settings even when they pretend to be realistic, symbolic settings for a timeless and unlocated (because internal) psychomachia." Overlooking the sweeping quality of Auden's observation, it is certainly true that in at least one very striking instance, the anonymous narrator whom we know only as Ishmael has a prototype in a well-known and widely read modern "realistic" novel: Robert Penn Warren's *All the King's Men*.

One of the reasons for the continuing popular success of Warren's novel since its appearance in 1946 (when it won the Pulitzer Prize) has been its recognizable politico-historical basis, as well as the rapid and melodramatic plot itself. The era of Huey Long is not so far behind us that the *roman à clef* element can be totally disregarded; furthermore, as a sociological study of southern political types and particularly of the American agrarian demagogue, the accuracy of Warren's rendering is noteworthy, and reminds us forcibly of the real world in which we exist. Both the Academy Award-winning motion picture version of the novel and the stage version stress the element emphasized on the cover of the paperback edition: "The world-famous American novel of power and corruption, and the meteoric rise and fall of Willie Stark—politician."

But it is as misleading to let this stand as a complete description of *All the King's Men* as it would be to say that *Moby-Dick* is a novel about whaling, or that *Hamlet* is a play about a young man who kills his uncle. Jack Burden, Warren's "Ishmael," at the end acknowledges the double nature of the tale he has told:

This has been the story of Willie Stark, but it is my story too. For I have a story. It is the story of a man who lived in the world and to him the world looked one way for a long time and then it looked another and very different way. The change did not happen all at once. Many things happened, and that man did not know when he had any responsibility for them and when he did not. There was, in fact, a time when he came to believe that nobody had any responsibility for anything and there was no god but the Great Twitch.

But as Jack Burden moves and struggles in the world of Willie Stark he eventually comes to accept the responsibility of being a human being, a responsibility which means involvement in "the convulsion of the world." The novel concludes "in the summer of this year, 1939," with Jack Burden finally ready to share the human burden as a mature and responsible adult. The events which began in late summer, 1939, suggest the world convulsion which Jack is now able to confront responsibly. An understanding of the world, a readiness to be engaged in it (instead of shrinking from it and interpreting everything as the meaningless Great Twitch), depends on understanding one's self—and this is what has happened to Jack.

A similar change takes place in Ishmael, although less explicitly defined. The opening paragraph of *Moby-Dick* depicts his condition prior to sailing on the *Pequod*. It is a period of the "damp, drizzly November" in his soul, when he is "grim about the mouth" and finds himself "involuntarily pausing before coffin warehouses, and bringing up the rear of every funeral" he meets. The gloomy, life-despairing Ishmael finds reflections of his own isolation everywhere he looks, in "the insular city of the 'Manhattoes' " and the *Pequod* as well—"Isolatoes too, I call such, not acknowledging the common continent of men, but each Isolato living on a separate continent of his own." The double pattern of action thereafter is to show Ishmael gradually rediscovering this common continent, while Ahab, in gaining diabolical control over his crewmen, alienates himself from mankind and is doomed to a "desolation of solitude" until his death.

Ishmael's progress in rediscovering the common continent is marked by several key incidents in the narrative. At first terror-stricken and horrified by being thrown together with the pagan

Queequeg, apparently as unlikely a representative of average humanity as one could hope to encounter, Ishmael soon discovers qualities
of sociability, friendship, and love binding them together. And when
Queequeg proffers his pipe and says that henceforth they are "married; meaning in his country's phrase, that we were bosom friends;
he would gladly die for me, if need should be," Ishmael is no longer
alone. (It is, significantly, Queequeg's buoyant coffin that paradoxically gives Ishmael life after the *Pequod* is sunk.) In that scene of the
monkey-rope, when Queequeg and Ishmael are tied together while
the harpooner dispatches a whale down in the ocean, Ishmael's reflection is that Queequeg is his "own inseparable twin brother; nor
could I any way get rid of the dangerous liabilities which the hempen
bond entailed." Brotherhood and responsibility, are bonds, but they
also may involve dangerous obligations from which man cannot
shrink. Both Ishmael and Jack Burden make this crucial discovery
which results in their salvation, while Ahab and Willie Stark refuse to
acknowledge it as truth. In a later scene which dramatizes the
Dickinson aphorism, "Much madness is divinest sense," Ishmael sits
with his crewmates squeezing lumps of sperm into fluid. This mind-
less occupation gradually arouses in him "abounding, affectionate,
friendly, loving" feelings, so that "at last I was continually squeezing
their hands and looking up into their eyes sentimentally; as much as
to say,—Oh! my dear fellow beings, why should we longer cherish
any social acerbities, or know the slightest ill-humor or envy! Come;
let us squeeze hands all around; nay, let us all squeeze ourselves into
each other; let us squeeze ourselves universally into the very milk and
sperm of kindness." The episode in which Ishmael, hypnotized by
the fierce glare of the tryworks, falls asleep at the tiller and reverses
his position, turning his back to the compass, dramatizes Ahab's
permanent posture, for Ahab is a man who has looked too long in
the face of the fire, a man who has discarded quadrant and compass.
Ishmael quotes the words of Solomon: "The man that wandereth out
of the way of understanding shall remain in the congregation of the
dead." It is Ishmael's fate—but not Ahab's—to return to the congregation of the living. After the *Pequod* goes down, Ishmael floats "on
a soft and dirge-like main," unharmed by sharks and savage sea-
hawks, until he is rescued by "the devious-cruising Rachel, that in
her retracing search after her missing children, only found another
orphan." Ishmael is brought back to the family of man. His experi-

ence at sea under Captain Ahab has been one of self-discovery; figuratively, he is reborn and (literally, also) he is saved.

Jack Burden is a student of history who balks at understanding
the past; he sees the experience but refuses to accept the meaning in
the story of Cass Mastern, his Ph.D. dissertation topic. As a result of
his refusal to face what the facts tell him, Jack drifts off into a career
of irresponsible isolationism, although ostensibly participating ac-
tively in the world as Willie Stark's assistant and leg-man. Much
later, Jack faces the meaning of the Cass Mastern story:

> Cass Mastern lived for a few years and in that time he
> learned that the world is all of one piece. He learned that
> the world is like an enormous spider web and if you touch
> it, however lightly, at any point, the vibration ripples to
> the remotest perimeter and the drowsy spider feels the
> tingle and is drowsy no more but springs out to fling the
> gossamer coils about you who have touched the web and
> then inject the black, numbing poison under your hide. It
> does not matter whether or not you meant to brush the
> web of things.

It is this sense of involvement, of the complexity of human relationships in a highly complex world, that Jack Burden flees from. To
him it is a "monstrous conspiracy," and he takes refuge in one of his
recurring periods of escapism to which he gives the name of the
Great Sleep. Jack refuses to acknowledge his common humanity;
that is, he acknowledges the presence of ugliness and evil in the
universe but insists on his own separateness and aloofness from them.
He does not shrink from evil, but he refuses to see that in order to be
human he must acknowledge the evil and guilt within himself. Like
Cass Mastern, he eventually learns that man cannot escape guilt,
even an unintended guilt.

Who killed Willie Stark? It was Dr. Adam Stanton, of course,
who fired the gun; but all—Adam, Tiny Duffy, Ann Stanton, Sadie
Burke, and Jack himself (not to omit Willie)—are partly responsible.
It is a shared guilt, the vibrations of the spider web involving all of
them. What shocks Jack most of all is that his role is unintended; that
is, in the interests of sterile factual research, he has also been responsible for Willie's murder. "It was as though I were caught in a more
monstrous conspiracy whose meaning I could not fathom." After

Willie's death, with Jack unwilling to accept the implications of his role, "I hated everything and everybody and myself and Tiny Duffy and Willie Stark and Adam Stanton. To hell with them all, I said impartially under the stars. They all looked alike to me then. And I looked like them." This recognition of his basic identification with the rest of ugly, corrupt, and incomplete humanity is what Jack Burden is struggling against.

Throughout the novel Jack takes refuge in a state of not-knowing, the Great Sleep being simply one variation. In the first chapter, he describes a state of tense anticipation using the image of a foetus:

> It wants to lie in the dark and not know, and be warm in
> its not-knowing. The end of man is knowledge, but there
> is one thing he can't know. He can't know whether
> knowledge will save him or kill him.

But man has to "open the envelope" in any event, "for the end of man is to know." Later after learning of Willie's affair with Ann, Jack flees to California, in an automatic gesture of recoil, "because when you don't like it where you are you always go west. . . . That was why I drowned in West." That this drowning, another attempt to return to the womb-state, solves no problems is evidenced by the fact that when he returns he still feels "at one with the Great Twitch" in a world where actions are neither good nor evil but meaningless, in a world out of time. As a history student who refuses to accept the past and who does not know his own past, Jack can have no concern about the future, and therefore the present is also meaningless. Jack creates his own insulated, sheltered, womb-state world.

That world, however, is cracked open when Jack Burden hears his mother scream one night—"a bright, beautiful, silvery soprano scream. I bounced off the bed and started for the door, realized that I was buck-naked, grabbed a robe, and ran out." Her involuntary cry of pain occurs when she finds that Jack's real father, Judge Irwin, has committed suicide (one of the other results of Jack's neutral "research"), and she accuses Jack of killing his father. But this moment inaugurates a change in Jack's vision of the world. Jack's rebirth is traumatic, but it begins to give him a new picture of his father (or rather gives him a picture of his new father) and a new understanding of his mother as a woman with a greater capacity for love than he had been willing to grant, rather than one "who loved merely power over men and the momentary satisfaction to vanity or flesh which they could give her, who lived in a strange loveless oscillation between calculation and instinct." What this rediscovery of his mother means is that, by giving him a new picture of herself, she can give him back the past "which I had before felt was tainted and horrible. I could accept the past now because I could accept her and be at peace with her and with myself." Jack's increase in understanding and acceptance of the world enables him also to be at peace with the Scholarly Attorney, the man he had previously thought was his father. When he discovers their true relationship, he can begin to accept the old man on altered terms, in a way that he could not before. Jack's reintegration is complete.

"There are two ways," Reinhold Niebuhr writes, "of denying our responsibilities to our fellowmen. The one is the way of imperialism, expressed in seeking to dominate them by our power. The other way is the way of isolationism, expressed in seeking to withdraw from our responsibilities to them." The irresponsibility of Jack Burden is an example of the latter kind; Willie Stark is clearly the example of domination. But what is the cause of Willie's downfall? It is, ironically, his "idealistic" decision to build a memorial hospital to his son Tom, free of the taint of such corrupt and grafting henchmen as Tiny Duffy and Gummy Larson. The key principle in Willie's career has been his recognition of the inseparability of abstractions like "good" and "evil," of the rejection of moral absolutes. He tells Adam Stanton that "goodness" has to be made "out of badness . . . And you know why? Because there isn't anything else to make it out of." Or, as he is fond of saying: "Man is conceived in sin and born in corruption and he passeth from the stink of the didie to the stench of the shroud." But Tom's death causes him to forget his guiding principle, and he becomes the victim of his attempt to divorce idealistic aspiration from brute corruption. Willie's monomaniacal obsession is of shorter duration and is less pervasive than Ahab's, but both are embodiments of the demon-ridden personality seeking transcendent absolutes. Each seeks to impose his own ideal upon nature; in so doing each alienates himself from common humanity and dies.

One of the reasons for the success of *All the King's Men,* as pointed out earlier, is the "realistic" picture of southern statehouse politics. Warren's novel is full of that "solidity of specification" which Henry James insisted on, "that merit on which all its other merits . . . helplessly and submissively depend." Likewise, one of the basic qualities in *Moby-Dick* (in addition to the element of excitement in the hunting of the whale) is that enumeration of factual detail found most obviously (but not exclusively) in the cetological chapters which have raised so many finicky critical eyebrows. These are recognizable everyday worlds created and inhabited by their narrators; the legislative machinations or whaling pursuits serve to define the principal boundaries and activities of those worlds. If the significance of the narrator's experience is that he sees meaning in rejoining the real world of human beings, then it is up to the artist to bring that world to life.

The rhetorical shifts which both authors employ as part of their strategy are also remarkably similar. Jack Burden's language alternates between the dry, unemotional reporting of the detached observer and the almost lyrical introspection of the tortured but ironical victim. In the former style, it is almost a parody of Hemingway:

> I hung the receiver up very deliberately, walked over to the desk and asked the clerk to give my bag to a bellhop, got a drink out of the lobby cooler, bought a couple of packs of cigarettes from the sleepy sister at the lobby stand, opened a package and lighted myself one, and stood there to take a long drag and look at the blank lobby, as though there weren't any place in the world where I had to go.

But this is Jack Burden, passive on his hotel bed, recapitulating history as he attempts to "drown in West":

> For that is where you come, after you have crossed oceans and eaten stale biscuits while prisoned forty days and nights in a stormy-tossed rat-trap, after you have sweated in the greenery and heard the savage whoop, after you have built cabins and cities and bridged rivers, after you have lain with women and scattered children like millet seed in a high wind, after you have composed resonant documents, made noble speeches, and bathed your arms in blood to the elbows, after you have shaken with malaria in the marshes and in the icy wind across the high plains. That is where you come, to lie alone on a bed in a hotel room in Long Beach, California. Where I lay, while outside my window a neon sign flickered on and off to the time of my heart,

systole and diastole, flushing and flushing again the gray
sea mist with a tint like blood.

It is important to note that the present Jack Burden, who recalls
the old Jack Burden, is employing alternating styles in order to re-
create and embody the two aspects of that un-integrated personality.
Seeing himself as from a distance, he even shifts pronouns in the long
sequence dealing with Jack Burden's university career, where it is not
"I" but "he"—the epitome of detachment.

The stylistic devices which Melville makes available to Ishmael
range also from factual registering of details concerning whale anat-
omy and the whaling industry to the Elizabethan rhetoric of the
dramatic soliloquies. It is not literal verisimilitude but imaginative
suggestiveness that Ishmael is aiming for; consequently, in his re-
construction of the whaling world he even includes incidents which,
strictly speaking, he cannot have seen. But these imaginative touches
constitute the liberty which an artist is entitled to take in order to
make more fully comprehensible the symbolic nature of his experience.

I do not suggest that Warren went to Melville for his model,
either consciously or unconsciously. But in the light of the remark-
able parallelisms between the two novels, the more than hundred
years of time between them seem little enough barrier to establish
their family resemblance. Ishmael and Jack Burden recreate for us an
archetypal pattern of human behavior, moving, as Aristotle has it,
from ignorance to knowledge—"the end of man is to know"—or
from isolation to common cause with mankind. The fate of the
proud man who steps outside of what Hawthorne called "the magnetic chain of humanity" is isolation, perhaps temporary dominion
and giddying power, but also self-torture and painful death. The fate
of the Ishmael-outcast who picks up his burden of human responsibilities and reenters the magnetic field is rebirth, love, and life.

The Metaphysics of Demagoguery: *All the King's Men*

Jonathan Baumbach

> *History is blind but man is not.*
> *All the King's Men*

Although Robert Penn Warren is a generation or so older than, with one exception, any of the writers treated in [*The Landscape of Nightmare*], he is technically a post–Second World War novelist. That is, the larger body of his fiction, including his major novel *All the King's Men,* has been published since 1945. Though a valuable novelist, Warren is also notably a playwright, poet, teacher, scholar, and critic—a man of letters in the best sense. The problem is, how does a man write a novel unself-consciously, when he is aware just how the critic, created perhaps in his own image, is likely to read it? The answer is, he doesn't. At least Warren doesn't.

Almost all of Warren's fiction suffers somewhat from the determined this-marriage-can-be-saved compatibility between Warren the novelist and Warren the explicator. The harder he tries to fuse the two selves, the farther apart they spring, as if resistant to the meddling of an outsider. As Eric Bentley has actually observed, "The problem lies precisely in his [Warren's] being so two-sidedly gifted; he evidently finds it endlessly difficult to combine his two sorts of awareness." Warren's novels are informed by a fairly complex set of intellectual alternatives, while at the same time they rely for their movement on frenetically charged melodramatic action, often for its

From *The Landscape of Nightmare: Studies in the Contemporary American Novel.* © 1965 by New York University. New York University Press, 1965.

own sake, for the sake merely of narrative excitement. Though Warren is a serious novelist, and at his best a brilliant prose writer, there is a curious separation in his novels between the events of the narrative and the meaning Warren insists they accommodate.

Of Warren's eight novels to date, *All the King's Men* (1946) seems to me the most achieved, the most serious and the most enduring—for all its flaws, one of our near-great novels. For some time *All the King's Men* was misread as a disturbingly sympathetic fictionalized account of the demagogic career of Huey Long. Approached as an historical document, the book was condemned by politically liberal critics as a florid, rhetorical justification for a Napoleonic brand of American neo-fascism. There is no need any longer to point out the irrelevancy of this attack, to explain that Jack Burden is the center of the novel and that Willie Stark, "the man of fact," is not *actually* Huey Long, but "Mistah Kurtz." In fact, in recent years a critical orthodoxy has clustered about Warren's novels, which is not unlike those contemporary angels headed by C. S. Lewis and Douglas Bush who guard the ages around Milton's *Paradise Lost,* protecting it from profanation by the infernal satanists. In both cases the defense is warranted; there is a real enemy. But in both cases the enemy is already within the gates. Though Warren intends Jack Burden to be the center of the novel, Willie Stark is by virtue of his energy the more realized and interesting character. Burden, as thinly disguised authorial spokesman, is a literary conception, created from other fiction rather than from life, a combination, if you can imagine it, of Nick Carraway and Sam Spade. Whatever Warren's intention, the character of Willie Stark, a colossus of human and inhuman possibilities, inadvertently dominates the novel. Inevitably, a distortion results, the kind of distortion which would permit *All the King's Men* to be read as the story of Willie Stark's rise and fall (a tragedy of over-reaching pride brought low by retributive justice).

For all that, Jack Burden, acquiescent narrator, at once vicarious Willie and vicarious Adam, is the novel's center, the ultimate synthesizer of its polarities. While Willie and Adam die unfulfilled, Jack completes the spiritual voyage; he moves, an exemplary sleepwalker, from sin to recognition and guilt to redemption and rebirth. Jack's ritual search for a true father, or at least a true absolute, leads him into Willie's employ (on the coattails of his political ascension). Ironically, there is a certain amount of narcissism in Jack's discipleship because he has, in part, created Willie the "Boss," catalyzed him from the raw materials of "Cousin Willie from the country." At the outset, Willie is an innocent, a do-gooder whose campaign speeches are scrupulously honest and drearily dull. Jack gives him his first taste of the apple:

> "Hell, make 'em cry, make 'em laugh, make 'em think you're God-Almighty. Or make 'em mad. Even mad at you. Just stir 'em up, it doesn't matter how or why, and they'll love you and come back for more. Pinch them in the soft place. They aren't alive, most of 'em haven't been alive in twenty years. Hell, their wives have lost their teeth and their shape, and likker won't set on their stomachs, and they don't believe in God, so it's up to you to give 'em something to stir 'em up and make 'em feel again. . . . But for Sweet Jesus' sake don't try to improve their minds.

This is the first and last time that Jack gives Willie a short course in cynical wisdom. Once having learned the lesson, Willie becomes the teacher, the authority on man's fallen nature. As Willie tells Jack later on in his (and Warren's) characteristic evangelical rhetoric: " 'Man is conceived in sin and born in corruption and passeth from the stink of the didie to the stench of the shroud. There is always something.' "

It is Jack, however, who has initiated Willie's conversion from the man of idea to the man of fact, from romanticism to pragmatism. By demonstrating to him that his start in politics was made possible by political corruption, Jack destroys Willie's sense of innocence, decreates him into manhood. While Jack, who suffers chronically from paralysis of the will, converts Willie through abstract example, Willie converts the uncommitted Jack through practical demonstration. The "Boss" Willie is Jack as he would like to be, but only if he could watch himself being it. For all his admiration of action, Jack is essentially a spectator, an historian waiting for history to happen. Willie performs history for him, tests the efficacy of Jack's theories, while Jack with clinical dispassion sits on the sidelines taking notes. (Jack's role as spectator is defined symbolically in the scene in which he sits in the hospital amphitheatre watching Adam Stanton perform a lobotomy.) As a dutiful son, Jack Burden participates in and even admires his father's ruthless pragmatism without sensing his own culpability. What you refuse to know can't hurt you, but, as Jack discovers, for only so long as you can remain blind. The longer you avoid self-knowledge, however, the more vulnerable you are to its intrusion.

Aside from Willie, Jack has two other fathers: a nominal one who he thinks is real and whom he has rejected (Ellis Burden) and a real one whom he admires and inadvertently kills (Judge Irwin). When Willie assigns him to get "something on" Judge Irwin, who has been outspoken in his criticism of Stark's administration, Jack is forced for the first time to choose between the prerogatives of opposing fathers. (Though he doesn't know that Irwin is his natural father, he respects, resents, and feels obligated to Irwin as a son to a father because of Irwin's decency and friendship over the years.) Looking for a way out of his predicament, Jack tells Willie that Irwin is "washed in the blood" and that an investigation of Irwin's past will be a waste of time. Willie knows, however, that man is fallen, that "there is always something." In investigating the facts of Irwin's life, Jack puts to the test the last illusion he has permitted himself to retain, that despite the rank and malodorous corruption which underlies so much of contemporary life, a truly good man like Irwin remains incorruptible. Jack has another naïve notion which justifies the political dirt-digging he does so that Willie can blackmail his opponents: that the truth, regardless of its immediate effects, is always salutary and that unadulterated fact constitutes truth.

In search of the hidden facts of his real father's past, Jack visits Ellis Burden, the Scholarly Attorney turned religious fanatic, his nominal father. It is here that the divergent influences of his trinity of fathers come into focus and are symbolically defined. Once again, Jack rejects the Scholarly Attorney, the weak saint, whose life of squalor, piety, and undiscriminating compassion seems purposeless to him when contrasted with Willie Stark's vigorous usefulness. This dispossessed nominal father has adopted a substitute son, George, a former circus aerialist who has reverted to childhood. George, redeemed through trauma into helpless innocence, spends his time making angels from masticated bread crusts. He is, in an ironic sense, Jack's brother. George's idiot purity embarrasses Jack and he rejects the image of his opposite (his innocent brother) along with his Scholarly Attorney father, along with the past. But, at the same time, he is again rejected by his father, who refuses to answer his questions about Irwin—who is unable to hear him when Jack calls him "Father." The visit is a failure; Jack learns nothing about Irwin, and he experiences the loss of his father all over again.

The uncovering of Irwin's one dishonorable act has massive, unaccountable ramifications. In consequence of Jack's discovery, Judge Irwin commits suicide, Anne Stanton has a self-destructive affair with Willie Stark, Adam Stanton kills Willie Stark, and Willie Stark's bodyguard kills Adam Stanton. For all his disinterested intentions, Jack must bear the burden of responsibility for this proliferation of tragedy. He has set it in motion as surely and perfectly as if he had consciously planned it. The "facts" that incriminate the Judge also indicate the complicity of Governor Stanton, who deliberately covered up for his friend. This further discovery destroys for both Anne and Adam Stanton the idealized notion of their father that has sustained them in their myth of purity as children of innocence—descendants of innocence. When Anne discovers that the purity of the old governor is tainted, she is able to shed her restrictive moral restraints as a snake sheds its skin. If there is no pure God, a pure Satan is the next best thing—he is at least whole. With the loss of her good father, Anne commits a sort of symbolic incest with the bad father—the new governor—searching for an absolute to replace the one she had lost. The loss of innocence in the novel for Jack, Willie, Anne, and Adam is concomitant with the loss of the good father.

It is Adam, Jack's innocent self, the least convincing of all Warren's characters, who guilelessly gives Jack his first lead in uncovering Irwin's blemished past. Adam answers Jack's cunning, direct question, "Was Judge Irwin ever broke?" because he is too ingenuous not to. However, Adams's innocent volunteering of harmless information about Judge Irwin is, in its effects, irresponsible as only innocence can be. It gives Jack the necessary clue to unearth Irwin's guilty secret, which, in ramification, destroys each of the participants in the central action of the novel. Adam's ingenuousness here anticipates his later, more destructive, act of innocence—his self-righteous assassination of Willie Stark. To say any more about Adam is beside the point. Whereas some of Warren's characters are half-human, half-idea, Adam is pure idea; he is an allegorical personification of *Innocence*. But without life, he is finally nothing, a figment of the author's imagination.

All of Warren's main characters experience at one time or another the loss of innocence and are characterized in terms of their accommodation to their Fall. Judge Irwin, sustained like Adam by the myth of self-purity, has attempted to evade the implications of his one intentionally corrupt act (his Fall) by shutting it out of his memory. Some thirty years later, Jack, the unacknowledged child of his loins, confronts him with the forgotten past. Jack's confrontation has a twofold significance; Jack is the manifestation of Irwin's other sin, his adulterous affair with Jack's mother, so that he becomes for Irwin the symbol of his fallen past, the tale-bearer of one crime and the embodiment of the other. Warren images Jack's information as a barb finding meat, suggesting its lethal nature. The Judge, illuminated by self-knowledge at once destructive and redemptive, bears his pain stoically. For a moment Irwin is tempted to reveal to his son the nature of their relationship in order that Jack withhold his information, but he doesn't—because it is beside the point.

> "I wouldn't hurt you," he said. Then, reflectively, added, "But I could stop you."
> "By stopping MacMurfee," I said.
> "A lot easier than that."
> "How?"
> "A lot easier than that," he repeated.
> "How?"
> "I could just . . ." he began, "I could just say to you— I could just tell you something. . . ." He stopped then suddenly rose to his feet, spilling the papers off his knees. "But I won't," he said cheerfully and smiled directly at me.

The moment of recognition is averted. By not telling Jack—an act of moral restraint—Irwin accepts full responsibility for his sin. Irwin's withholding of his "truth" is, given the occasion, more honorable than Jack's revelation of his. The next morning Jack is awakened by his mother's "bright, beautiful silvery soprano screams." In her hysteria, she continues to shriek at Jack, " 'You killed him, you killed him,' " without identifying the "him": " 'Killed who?' I demanded, shaking her. 'Your father,' she said, 'your father and oh! you killed him.' "

Without further clarification, Jack realizes what has happened, as if he had known all the time, in the secret wisdom of instinct, that Irwin was his father. That the Judge shoots himself through the heart indicates symbolically the implication of Jack's betrayal. Despite the terrible consequences of his act, Jack reflects on his responsibility for Irwin's suicide, as if it were an intellectual abstraction which does not touch him personally. At first he considers his father's death as the just retribution of Mortimer Littlepaugh, the man whom Irwin's own corrupt act drove to suicide. Then:

> Or had it been Mortimer? Perhaps I had done it. That was one way of looking at it. I turned that over and speculated upon my responsibility. It would be quite possible to say that I had none, no more than Mortimer had. Mortimer had killed Judge Irwin because Judge Irwin had killed him and I killed Judge Irwin because Judge Irwin had created me, and looking at matters in that light one could say that Mortimer and I were only the twin instruments of Irwin's protracted and ineluctable self-destruction. For either killing or creating may be a crime punishable by death, and the death always comes by the criminal's own hand and every man is a suicide. If a man knew how to live he would never die.

It is a characteristically easy rationalization for Jack, one which enables him to avoid for a time the implications of his behavior. Like every man, he too is a suicide (though a moral rather than a physical one) and, ultimately, ineluctably, his sins revisit him like retributive ghosts. As a result of Irwin's death, Jack loses two fathers, the weak but saintly Scholarly Attorney and the strong but tainted judge. Willie Stark, the evil father, the father who has cuckolded him, is all that is left for Jack in a world of decimated fathers, and finally Jack kills him too. As Jack tells us, " 'I had dug up the truth and the truth always kills the father.' " In a symbolic sense, only after Jack destroys his fathers can he become a man himself. As part of his quest for knowledge (manhood), Jack kills the fathers of his world only to resurrect them finally in himself.

Jack's articulated intellection dissipates the effect of this scene as it does much of the richly rendered experience of the novel. Granted his cleverness, Jack is verbally aware of too much, and also too little; Warren is forever peeking over his shoulder, but withholding from his narrator the whole picture. That Jack as narrator is almost always the deception of an insight ahead of the reader is one of the recurring distractions of the novel. With rare exception, the reader is not permitted to discover meanings; they are discovered for him.

When Willie loses his innocence, he is transformed almost overnight from the son of his world to its father. Willie's spiritual metamorphosis (which resembles Kurtz's in *Heart of Darkness*), though thematically subordinate to Jack's guilt-and-redemption passage, dominates the action of the novel. Willie's career anticipates and parallels Jack's, as a father's anticipates a son's, though it is enlarged where Jack's is diminished, and Willie never successfully makes the spiritual voyage back from hell. Like Kurtz, the "Boss" has gone too far into darkness ever to return into light.

Willie becomes governor. Ostensibly, his ends have not changed, only his means of achieving them. Gradually, however, the ends become inseparable from their means and Willie yields himself to his most voracious interior devils. The thesis is classic and bromidic: power tends to corrupt; absolute power tends to corrupt absolutely. With a difference, however: Warren inverts the cliché; for all his sins, "Willie is a great man." This is the verdict of his wife Lucy, to whom he has been unfaithful, whose son he has destroyed through vanity, and of Jack Burden, whom he has disillusioned and nearly destroyed. Since the redeemed Jack Burden, who has moved from blindness to whole sight represents, one must believe, the point of view of the novel, this must stand as Warren's judgment of Stark. The question remains: Is it a reasonable judgment borne out by the experience of the novel? Or is it a piece of gratuitous iconoclasm, the cliché-anti-cliché?

Warren enlists sympathy for Willie by indicating that the context in which he is forced to operate (southern politics) is unreclaimably corrupt. Whereas Tiny Duffy and Willie's opponent MacMurfee are interested in petty graft as an end, Willie's ego wants nothing less than recognition by posterity. Willie is a real devil at sup among dwarfed, flabby devils; in that he is more real and more potent than the others, he is to that extent more admirable. Once Willie has fallen, he discovers his true voice, the voice of the rabble rouser, the appeal to primordial violence:

> "You asked me what my program is. Here it is, you hicks. And don't you forget it. Nail 'em up! Nail up Joe Harrison. Nail up anybody who stands in your way. Nail up MacMurfee if he don't deliver. You hand me the hammer and I'll do it with my own hand. Nail 'em up on the barn door."

The easier it becomes for Willie to manipulate the crowd, the less respect he has for its common fallen humanity. As he becomes more powerful, he becomes, like Kurtz and like Macbeth, more voracious, more proud, more evil. Willie's palpable moral decline is manifested for us when he covers up for an underling who has taken graft. It is not in the act of covering up but in his justification for it that Willie's inhumanity and presumption are manifested:

> "My God, you talk like Byram was human! He's a thing! You don't prosecute an adding machine if a spring goes bust and makes a mistake. You fix it. Well, I fixed Byram. I fixed Byram. I fixed him so his unborn great-grand-children will wet their pants on this anniversary and not know why. Boy, it will be the shock in the genes. Hell, Byram is just something you use, and he'll sure be useful from now on."

Willie's self-defining presumption is that he *knows* himself a superior being, aspiring to law, to omnipotence, to God. The machine metaphor he employs reveals his attitude not only toward Byram but toward the populace in general: people are things to be used by him, "the Boss," for *his* purposes. From Willie's "bulging-eyed" point-of-view, everything, all existence, has been set in motion to serve him.

Willie's will to power, his lust for omnipotence, is defeated by what might be called a tragic virtue. Despite Willie's professed thesis that "you have to make the good out of the bad because that's all you have to make it out of," that all men are innately corrupt, that "political graft is the grease that keeps the wheels from squeaking," he wants to build a magnificent, immaculate hospital as his gift to the state, untainted by the usual petty corruption and graft. In pursuing this ideal, Willie refuses a deal with Gummy Larson, the power behind his enemy MacMurfee, whose defection to Willie would leave the "Boss" all but unopposed. Having fallen from Paradise into Hell, Willie wishes—his one romantic illusion—to regain his lost purity, to buy back Paradise. Willie tries to explain his motives to Jack:

> "Can't you understand either? I'm building that place, the best in the country, the best in the world, and a bugger like Tiny is not going to mess with it, and I'm going to call it the Willie Stark Hospital and it will be there a long time after I'm dead and gone and you are dead and gone and all those sons-of-bitches are dead and gone and anybody, no matter he hasn't got a dime, can go there . . ."

> "And will vote for you," I said.
> "I'll be dead," he said, "and you'll be dead, and I don't
> care whether he votes for me or not, he can go there and
> . . ."
> "And bless your name," I said.

That Willie, so compellingly articulate on other occasions, cannot cogently rationalize his motives suggests that they are contradictory to him as well as to Jack. He wants at once to be noble and to have everyone admire his nobility—selflessness for the sake of self. Yet, and herein lies the contradiction, he also wants redemption.

As part of his obsessive desire to transcend his corruption, his dream of greatness, Willie hires Adam Stanton to run his hospital, hoping through connection, through transfusion of spirit, to inform himself with Adam's innocence. Ironically, Willie has, with almost perfect instinct, chosen his redeemer, his redeemer as executioner. Adam and Willie as ideological polarities must inevitably merge or destroy each other. Jack unites them; he is the means of their collaborative self-destruction.

Willie's brief affair with Adam's sister Anne, is another extension of his specious quest for innocence. What Willie pursues is not innocence, really, but seeming innocence—respectability. His holy search for the false grail is the tragic flaw in his otherwise perfect expediency. Willie's lost innocence resides not with Adam and Anne, but with his wife Lucy and his father; his substitution of Anne for Lucy symbolizes his degeneration, his spiritual blindness. In his obsession with purity, Willie makes an enemy of the spiteful Tiny Duffy and puts too much faith in the erratically naïve, the fallen innocent, Adam, thereby predicating his own destruction. Duffy makes an anonymous phone call to Adam, falsifying the implications of Anne's affair with Willie. The inflexibly idealistic Adam, unable to live in an imperfect world, acts as the unwitting tool of vengeful petty corruption and gratuitously murders Willie. Specious innocence and cowardly corruption conspire to destroy the "Boss" at the height of his power and at the threshold of his apparent self-reform.

Willie's deathbed scene is the most potent of the various dramatic climaxes in the novel. In it Warren brings sharply into focus the moral paradox of Willie's ethic—the tragedy of his unachieved, over-reaching ambition; it is rendered as Judge Irwin's death is not, as a profoundly affecting experience. It is the death of Jack's last symbolic father—in extension of all his fathers—leaving him, for a time, alone and uncommitted in the chaos of his ungoverned universe. I quote the scene at length because it is a resonant fusion of idea and action, a moment of illumined truth.

> For a minute he didn't speak but his eyes looked up at me, with the light still flickering in them. Then he spoke: "Why did he do it to me?"
>
> "Oh, God damn it," I burst out, very loud, "I don't know."
>
> The nurse looked warningly at me.
>
> "I never did anything to him," he said.
>
> "No, you never did."
>
> He was silent again, and the flicker went down in his eyes. Then, "He was all right. The Doc."
>
> I nodded.
>
> I waited, but it began to seem that he wasn't going to say any more. His eyes were on the ceiling and I could scarcely tell that he was breathing. Finally, the eyes turned toward me again, very slowly, and I almost thought that I could hear the tiny painful creak of the balls in their sockets. But the light flickered up again. He said "It might have been all different, Jack."
>
> I nodded again.
>
> He roused himself more. He even seemed to be straining to lift his head from the pillow. "You got to believe that," he said hoarsely.
>
> The nurse stepped forward and looked significantly at me.
>
> "Yes," I said to the man on the bed.
>
> "You got to," he said again. "You got to believe that."
>
> "All right."
>
> He looked at me, and for a moment it was the old strong, probing, demanding glance. But when the words came this time, they were very weak. "And it might have been different yet," he whispered. "If it hadn't happened, it might—have been different—even yet."

Willie's deathbed claim is an easy one to make; it is as impossible to prove as to disprove. One is tempted to say to him, as Jake does to Brett at the end of *The Sun Also Rises,* "Isn't it pretty to think so?"

though significantly Jack does not. However, it is not out of motives of sentiment that Jack withholds his ironic disbelief. He is not fully convinced that Willie's self-justification is unjust. The possibility remains: "It might have been different—even yet." Willie is, after all, a paradox.

In becoming Willie's executioner, Adam, in his blind way, follows the example of Willie's career—he becomes Willie. For the "man of fact" and the "man of idea," as Jack classified them, there has been an alternation of roles. Each incomplete, seeking completeness, has chosen his polar opposite as an exemplary image. In building the hospital without the "grease" of political graft, Willie is operating idealistically—in Adam's image. In brutally shooting down Willie, Adam is acting as disciple of the man whose power-authority is symbolized by the meat axe. From Jack's standpoint, Willie is superior to Adam: "A man's virtue may be but the defect of his desire, as his crime may be but a function of his virtue." If a man has not faced temptation, or, as in Adam's case, has not admitted its existence, his purity is illusory and beside the point.

Willie's relationship to his son Tom is another variation on the novel's father–son conflict, and it serves as an ironic comment both on Jack's relationship to his real father and to Willie. Jack's search into Irwin's discreditable past is continually juxtaposed to scenes of Willie worshipfully watching Tom perform on the football field: " 'He's my boy—and there's not any like him—he'll be All-American.' " Tom Stark is the perfect physical extension of Willie's wishful self-image; he is all man of action—with the bottle, on the gridiron, and in bed—one hundred percent performance, no waste. Burden sees his as "one hundred and eighty pounds of split-second, hair trigger, Swiss-watch beautiful mechanism." Inhuman but perfect, he is the embodiment of Willie's crass values. Willie is willing to overlook Tom's personal decay so long as he continues to function as a perfect mechanism on the football field and so sate Willie's rapacious vanity. Willie's attitude toward Tom is symbolic of his attitude toward the governmental machine—proud, permissive, and blind. Corruption is permissible because it "keeps the wheels from squeaking." His failure with Tom is symptomatic of his potential failure as governor; to satisfy his vanity Willie would have all men, even his own son, made into functioning "things." Inadvertently, Willie destroys Tom, who is, outside of personal power, the "thing" he loves most in his world. When Tom has been barred from playing football for breaking college rules (the boy manages, among his heroics, to cripple one girl in an auto crash and to impregnate another), Willie pressures the coach into reinstating him. Almost immediately after Tom comes into the game, as if in direct consequence of Willie's corrupt use of authority, his spine is snapped by a vicious tackle. As a result, the son of the man-of-action is left actionless, without the use of his arms and legs. As the emotional paralysis of Jack catalyzes, in a sense, the action of Willie, Willie's action causes the physical paralysis of Tom. The irony is evident: ultimately a machine stops, even a perfect Swiss-made mechanism breaks down if it is dropped too often. The sins of the father are visited on the son. Similarly, the "breaking" of the son anticipates the destruction of the father; it is an intimation of Willie's mortality.

Whereas in Jack's case the son kills the father, in Willie's the father kills the son. However, Tom is, through the ineluctable chain of cause and effect, also the instrument of Willie's destruction. As a consequence of Tom's impregnating the daughter of one of MacMurfee's men, Willie is forced through blackmail to compromise his principles and give the corrupt Gummy Larson the hospital-construction contract. After Tom's injury, however, the guilt-ridden Willie breaks the contract. Tiny Duffy, who has been intermediary in the deal, exacts his vengeance; he initiates Willie's murder through Adam's pride.

Before Adam shoots him down, Willie accepts Tom's paralysis as a judgment for his sins and seeks expiation through good works: "you got to start somewhere." As Irwin ultimately redeems Jack, Tom almost redeems Willie, but not quite; after his fall, Humpty-Dumpty cannot be put together again. Willie, like Tom's paralyzed body, is denied rebirth. Willie's death does, however, make possible the redemption of Tom's illegitimate son, whom Lucy decides to adopt and name, of all names, Willie Stark. Through his son's son, Willie regains his lost innocence.

With the death of Willie, the effective father, Jack has no one left to whom he can transfer his responsibility. However, before he can achieve manhood, Jack has one other father with whom he has to come to terms—Cass Mastern; the subject of his Ph.D. dissertation is Jack's historic father. The episode of Cass Mastern, a self-contained short story within the novel, is intended as a gloss (in Warren's term, "the myth") on the larger action of the main narrative. Though it illuminates certain themes in *All the King's Men* and is in itself an exceptionally resonant tale, Cass's tragedy is hardly indispensable to the novel. In any event, at the cost of temporarily stopping the action, it gives added dimension to Burden's odyssey into self-knowledge, his passage from innocence to limbo to guilt to redemption. Though Jack has pieced together all the facts of Cass Mastern's life, he is unable to complete his dissertation. The significance of Cass's story eludes him, though he is aware that it has significance. Neither Jack's early philosophic idealism ("What you don't know won't hurt you") nor his disillusioned belief in the Great Twitch (that man is an involuntary mechanism and no one is responsible for anything) is adequate to a comprehension of Cass's sainthood. Cass, though innocent and virtuous, falls into an affair with Annabell Trice, his best friend's wife. As a consequence, three lives are destroyed. Thereafter Cass, suffused with guilt, makes his existence a continuous penance for his sin. He finally joins the Southern army and gives up his life while refusing to fire a shot in his own defense. Through martydom he achieves expiation. At the end, Cass becomes a religious fanatic, and on his deathbed he sends a strange letter to his successful brother. The passage is typical of the evangelical eloquence of Warren's rhetoric:

> Remember me, but without grief. If one of us is lucky, it is I. I shall have rest and I hope in the mercy of the Everlasting and his blessed election. But you, my dear brother, are condemned to eat bread in bitterness and build on the place where the charred embers and ashes are and to make bricks without straw and to suffer in the ruin and guilt of our dear Land and in the common guilt of man.

Cass's martyrdom is exemplary; it is not only his own guilt for which he has suffered and died but the guilt of the land, "the common guilt of man." In the mystery of Cass's life and death resides the meaning of Jack's life, which is to say the essential meaning of all our lives. As Cass has written in his journal, and as Jack finally discovers for himself, " 'It is a human defect—to try to know oneself by the self of another. One can only know oneself in God and His great eye.' " After the recognition of his guilt, it is in God that Cass does find himself; similarly, after Jack accepts his guilt, it is in himself that he finds Cass and, ultimately, God. The recognition of guilt for Cass (and by implication for Jack) is an awesome discovery.

It was, instead, the fact of all these things—the death of my friend, the betrayal of Phoebe, the suffering and rage and great change of the woman I had loved—all had come from my single act of sin and perfidy, as the boughs from the bole and the leaves from the bough. Or to figure the matter differently, it was as though the vibration set up in the whole fabric of the world by my act had spread infinitely and with ever increasing power and no man could know the end. I did not put it into words in such fashion, but I stood there shaken by a tempest of feeling.

Cass's revelation is existential; that is, since the ramifications of a particular act are for the most part unknowable and the inherent responsibility for its entire chain reaction inescapable, the burden of guilt is endless—and unbearable. So Cass, in search of redemption, tracks down the various consequences of his act of sin only to discover that there is no undoing of the harm he has already caused. What he has done is irrevocable. It is only by "living in God's eye"—a saint's life—that he can hope to achieve expiation and redemption.

Since Duncan Trice, who is considerably older than Cass, initiates him into vice, he is, in effect, the father of Cass's adultery with Annabelle. What Cass has learned from Duncan he had put into practice with Duncan's wife. Therefore, Cass's crime, Warren suggests, is implicitly incestuous, for if Duncan, the man whose death he effects, is his "substitute" father, Anabelle as his wife is a sort of symbolic mother. This is essentially what Cass understands when he proclaims himself " 'the chief of sinners and a plague spot on the body of the human world.' "

Cass's experience acts as an anticipatory parallel to Jack's own nightmare passage, though the connections are remote and abstract. When Jack discovers that Duffy "had killed Stark as surely as though his own hand had held the revolver," he feels absolved of responsibility, free at last to act, to vindicate the deaths of Willie and Adam. However, Jack's newborn sense of freedom is illusory. It is for him another evasion of responsibility, in a way the least admirable of all. Convincing himself as Willie had, and as Adam had when he squeezed the trigger, that an act is a self-willed moral entity, Jack assumes for himself the role of avenging angel; he wishes to destroy Duffy in order to justify himself. However, after Jack chastises Duffy, " 'You are the stinkingest louse God ever let live!' " and threatens him with

exposure, he realizes that " 'I had tried to make Duffy into a scape-
goat for me and to set myself off from Duffy,' " that Duffy is his
alter ego, his corrupt brother, and that whatever he had said about
Duffy was also true of himself. In the power of Warren's prose, we
get the visceral horror of Jack's self-revulsion:

> It was as though in the midst of the scene Tiny Duffy had
> slowly and like a brother winked at me with his oyster eye
> and I had known he knew the nightmare truth, which was
> that we were twins bound together more intimately and
> disastrously than the poor freaks of the midway who are
> bound by the common stitch of flesh and gristle and the
> seepage of blood. We were bound together forever and I
> could never hate him without hating myself or love myself
> without loving him.
>
> And I heaved and writhed like the ox or the cat, and the
> acid burned my gullet and that's all there was to it and I
> hated everybody and myself and Tiny Duffy and Willie
> Stark and Adam Stanton.

Jack, by evading the responsibility for his own sins, had, amid
the corruption about him, retained the illusion of innocence. Since he
had not acted out of conscious choice, but had merely yielded to the
demands of the "Boss," he had been able to slough off the burden of
guilt. Once he discovers himself free to act, he becomes aware that
the possibility of all acts, the whole spectrum of good and evil, are in
him; that he is, as human being, Oedipus and Duffy and Willie and
everyone else. Having discovered the magnitude of his guilt—that he
is responsible not only for his own sins but for all sins—Jack begins
his return from the interior hell in which he has languished so long.
He cannot leave hell, of course, until he has discovered its boundaries.

When Jack runs into "Sugar-Boy," Willie's driver and bodyguard (*the* man of action), he is presented with the opportunity of
destroying Duffy with no risk to himself. He restrains himself not
out of the paralysis ("the defect of desire") which prevented him
many years before from making love to Anne when she offered
herself to him but because Duffy is his "twin," and if he can sanction
Duffy's murder he must sanction his own. (Cass refused to kill in the
Civil War because: " 'How can I, who have taken the life of my
friend, take the life of an enemy, for I have used up my right to

blood?' ") Jack's refusal to take easy vengeance on Duffy is not inaction but a decisive moral act.

For a time, as a projection of his self-hate, Jack has a baleful view
of all humanity. When he comes to love his mother, whom he has
rejected long ago, he is able as a consequence to stop hating himself,
which also means no longer hating the rest of the world. The redemption of his mother through the recognition of her love for Irwin
(his real father) is Jack's salvation; it reestablishes for him the existential possibility of love. However, as Jack discovers, the process
has been circular, for " 'by killing my father I have saved my mother's soul.' " This discovery leads Jack into a further revelation (which
is Warren's thesis) that " 'all knowledge that is worth anything is
maybe paid for by blood.' "

For all his belief in the purgative powers of knowledge, Jack lies
to his mother when she asks about the motive for Irwin's suicide,
telling her that his father killed himself because of failing health. It is,
however, a salutary lie, the least he can do for his mother. As his
mother's rebirth has resurrected him, Jack's lie resurrects the image
of his father for his mother. (Jack's withholding of the truth from his
mother closely parallels Marlowe's lie to Kurtz's intended at the end
of *Heart of Darkness.* In both cases the lie is noble, and, in a sense, the
truth.) His reconciliation with his mother begins his reconciliation
with the past. For without the past Jack cannot really participate in
the world of the present. By rediscovering the past he is able to
re-create the present, to be spiritually reborn into a world in which
before his destructive self-awareness he had only acquiescently participated. He moves into his father's house, affirming his linear her-
itage, accepting for himself at last the role of man and father. He
marries his boyhood sweetheart Anne Stanton, to whom he had once
in love and innocence committed his life irrevocably. In marrying
Anne, Jack saves her in much the same way Pip saves Estella at the
end of *Great Expectations.* Anne is the symbol to him of his lost
innocence, and in redeeming her he at last redeems himself. Having
accepted the past with its hate and love, its guilt and pride, its evil
and good, Jack can be regenerated into the world of the present,
redeemed through suffering and self-knowledge.

When Stark and Adam destroy each other, Jack emerges from
the vicarious experience of their deaths as the synthesis of their alternatives, as a whole man. Through the responsibility his manhood
imposes on him, he brings the Scholarly Attorney, old and dying,

into his home. Finally, it is the old man, the religious fanatic, the "unreal" father from whom Jack learns the ultimate facts of life, who becomes a "real" father. ("Each of us is the son of a million fathers.") Jack comes to believe in the old man's religious doctrine that " 'the creation of evil is . . . the index of God's glory and His power. That had to be so that the creation of good might be the index of man's glory and power. But by God's help. By His help and His wisdom.' "

Through his "father," Jack is able to understand the significance of Cass Mastern's life in the "eye of God." After Jack's nominal father dies and he has completed his study of Cass Mastern, fulfilling at last all of his obligations to the past, he can leave Judge Irwin's house, the womb of his rebirth, and "go into the convulsion of the world, out of history into history and the awful responsibility of time." While Cass has sacrificed his life to redeem himself, Jack achieves redemption somewhat easily and painlessly. For this reason, Jack's ultimate salvation seems externally imposed (redemption as happy ending), abstract and literary rather than real. Yet to object to Warren's fine novel because it falls short of its potentialities seems finally presumption. To have it better than it is would be at the expense of gambling with what it has already achieved—a fool's risk. *All the King's Men* is a great scarred bear of a book whose faults and virtues determine one another. The greatness of this bear devolves upon the magnificence of its faults and the transcendence into art of its palpable mortality.

Robert Penn Warren: *All the King's Men*

Arthur Mizener

Robert Penn Warren has had at least four careers as a writer. He has written six volumes of poems, one of which, *Promises,* won him the Pulitzer Prize in 1957; his *Selected Poems* won the Bollingen award for 1966. He had already received the Pulitzer Prize for fiction in 1946 with *All the King's Men,* the third of his eight novels. He has written a biography of John Brown and two books on segregation. He has been one of the important contributors to the critical renaissance of the twentieth century and found (with Cleanth Brooks) a way to make its insights available to students in the most influential text-book of our time, *Understanding Poetry.* There is something symbolic about this last achievement, for the most persistent of Mr. Warren's beliefs is that men must, at whatever cost, carry knowledge into the world, must live their daily lives by its lights and must subject it to the test of experience.

Mr. Warren is usually thought of as a member of the Fugitive Group that gathered in the 1920s at Vanderbilt, where the young Warren studied with John Crowe Ransom and roomed for a time with Allen Tate. It is difficult to imagine a better apprenticeship in the craft of writing than working with Ransom, and to have been exposed to the grace, the wit, and the violence of Allen Tate's mind must have been almost too stimulating. Yet the association of War-ren with the Fugitives is misleading, too. There were other impor-tant influences in his life, at California and Yale and Oxford, where he did graduate work, and wherever it was that he acquired the

From *The Southern Review* 3 (1967). © 1967 by Arthur Mizener.

attitude—very different from either Ransom's or Tate's—that he has always had.

The starting point for that attitude—as for the different one taken by Tate—is the problem of self-realization and self-possession. The speaker in Tate's "Ode to the Confederate Dead" can

> praise the vision
> And praise the arrogant circumstance
> Of those who fall
> Rank upon rank, hurried beyond decision,

but they are not real to him; he cannot share their vision or even truly understand it, though for a moment of pious respect for the past he imagines them rising like demons out of the earth. What is real for him is their tombstones, as neatly aligned as their ranks had been, decaying slowly in a neutral air.

> Row after row with strict impunity
> The headstones yield their names to the element,
> The wind whirs without recollection

in a world where impunity is absolute and the idea of meaningful action ("yielding") a pathetic fallacy. The conception of nature that had given the lives of these Confederate dead coherence and value is gone. "Here by the sagging gate, stopped by the wall" of the cemetery, the speaker feels a despair at his situation that is intensified by his recognition of what the world buried there, and long since reduced by time to "verdurous anonymity," had been like. (Tate particularly likes barriers that emphasize the metaphysical impenetrability he is concerned with by their physical insignificance; the mirror of "Last Days of Alice" is even more striking than the sagging gate of the "Ode," in which a version of that mirror in fact also turns up in the passage about the jaguar that "leaps / For his own image in a jungle pool, his victim.") For Tate the cost of losing an endurable vision of nature is the loss of the world; deprived of the vision of a community and its discipline, the individual sinks into the incoherent abyss of impulse where

> You shift your sea-space blindly
> Heaving, turning like the blind crab.

This is the nightmare in which George Posey, the hero of Tate's novel, *The Fathers,* exists. "But," says the narrator of *The Fathers,* "is not civilization the agreement, slowly arrived at, to let the abyss alone?" Tate's image of the civilized man is the narrator's father, Major Buchan, whose feelings have been perfectly disciplined to the expressive social ritual of antebellum life at Pleasant Hill. There is in *The Fathers* an understanding that a civilization is subject to time and change: George Posey destroys the life of Pleasant Hill even before the Civil War destroys the social system it is a part of. But for Tate that change is simply an occasion for despair, for the recognition that we can never be Major Buchan, only George Posey.

To Warren the world of our time seems a convulsion quite as terrible as it is for Tate. But for him the world exists beyond any conception of it we may have; and it always has. We cannot know the past—but only some destructive conception of it—until we recognize that Willie Stark of *All the King's Men* is right when he says of it, "I bet things [then] were just like they are now. A lot of folks wrassling around." That knowledge about the past does not make the past meaningless, any more than does the knowledge that for the same reason we will never create a Utopia makes the future meaningless. It only makes the past and future real.

In one of the several poems Mr. Warren has written about the maternal grandfather (he was a cavalry officer under Forrest) who is his Major Buchan, the grandson begins by thinking that

> life is only a story
> And death is only the glory
> Of the telling of the story,
> And the *done* and the *to-be-done*
> In that timelessness were one,
> Beyond the poor *being done*.

Then his grandfather describes how he and his men once hanged a group of bushwackers, and suddenly the boy understands that his grandfather's past life was not a story, not something that exists only as a timeless *done* but something that was once *being done* in the terrible now of time:

> Each face outraged, agape,
> Not yet believing it true—
> The hairy jaw askew,
> Tongue out, out-staring eye,

> And the spittle not yet dry
> That was uttered with the last cry.
>
> The horseman does not look back.
> Blank-eyed, he continues his track,
> Riding toward me there,
> Through the darkening air.
>
> The world is real. It is there.

But it is very tempting to deny that the life of the past took place in the real world of time, as life in the present does, and to reject the life of the present as inconceivable in the light of what one imagines the past to have been. That is what Adam Stanton in *All the King's Men* does all his life; it is what Jack Burden, the novel's narrator, does for a long time, so that when, for example, he meets the sheriff and Commissioner Dolph Pillsbury in the Mason City court house, he wants to believe such creatures do not exist. With repudiating irony he tells himself that Dolph Pillsbury is "just another fellow, made in God's image and wearing a white shirt with a ready-tied black bow tie and jean pants held up with web galluses." But he knows Dolph Pillsbury is real, even if he won't admit it to himself (it is the Jack Burden who tells the story, long afterwards, who does admit it): "*They ain't real,* I thought as I walked down the hall [of the courthouse], *narry one.* But I knew they were."

It is not that man does not need a vision of the ideal possibilities of life or that actual life does not often seem grotesquely horrible in comparison with that vision. It is not even that, for some men, it is not altogether too easy to accept the world as it is and forget its unrealized possibilities (as Willie Stark for a while does). The danger is that men who do not forget these possibilities may, like Jack Burden, refuse to understand that they are possibilities for the world and are real only in the world. The risk of trying to realize these possibilities in the world is destruction, but not to take that risk is never to live. "For if," as Shakespeare's duke says, "our virtues / Did not go forth of us, 'twere all alike / As if we had them not." (There are interesting similarities between *All the King's Men* and Shakespeare's "dark" comedies, *Measure for Measure* and *Troilus and Cressida*.) But it is temptingly easy, too, to think that one must not enter the grotesque reality of the world if one has any virtues.

When, in *Flood,* a prison guard refuses to shoot a madman who is murdering another guard for fear of hitting an innocent man, the Warden says, "Jesus Christ, a innocent man! There ain't no innocent man! You are fired." Yet it remains true, as the novel's cultivated lawyer says, that "when I look out the window and see some pore misguided boogers doing the best they can—according to their dim lights . . . what you might call the pathos of the mundane sort of takes the edge off my grim satisfaction." No man can afford not to shoot a murderous madman on the theory that the bystanders who are sure to be hurt are innocent (no man is) or on the theory that, since no man is innocent, men are not worth his trouble. Both theories assume that one is innocent oneself and that this innocence can be preserved by avoiding the infection of a world that is not. But the world is made up of men just like us, guilty men in ready-tied bow ties and jean pants, certainly; and made in God's image, too.

For Mr. Warren the worst is not to go into the convulsion of the world, terrible as it is to do that. No one in fact exists anywhere else. But men can deprive themselves of the responsibility (and the freedom) of being there by refusing to submit their virtues to the test of action, as Jack Burden does, or by acting as if virtue does not exist, as do the host of small-time pursuers of happiness who people Mr. Warren's novels, such as Marvin Frey, "a sporting barber with knife-edge creases in his striped pants, ointment on his thinning hair, hands like inflated rubber gloves. . . . You know how he kids the hotel chippies and tries to talk them out of something, you know how he gets in debt because of his bad hunches on the horses and bad luck with the dice, you know how he wakes up in the morning and sits on the edge of the bed with his bare feet on the cold floor and a taste like brass on the back of his tongue and experiences his nameless despair."

"Mentre che la speranza ha fior del verde," says the epigraph of *All the King's Men* ("Per lor maladizione sì non si perde / che non possa tornar l'etterno amore, / mentre che la speranza ha fior del verde. [By their curse none is so lost that the eternal love cannot return while hope keeps any of it green.]" *Purgatorio* 3.133–35). In this canto, Dante sees his shadow and Virgil, confessing he is lost, knows he must consult the penitents. Sinclair observes that Dante's casting a shadow "illustrate[s] the dualism of flesh and spirit . . . which is not to be resolved in theory, only in experience"; and of Virgil consulting the penitents, he says, "In this need penitence is wiser than reason, and reason is then most reasonable when it looks beyond itself. The soul's life is experience, a given thing—a *quia,* in the language of scholasticism—to be known only in living, in the last resort as unsearchable as God." ("State contenti, umana gente, al *quia,*" 1.37.)

One of Mr. Warren's major objects in *All the King's Men* is to make the world of time in which experience occurs exist for us in all its ordinary, familiar, immediate reality. The novel's story of the typical political struggle in which the country boy, Willie Stark, rose to power and of his exercise of that power, of the career of Judge Irwin of Burden's Landing with its judicial integrity, its marriage for money, its deal with the power company—this story is representative of the public life of our time. It occurs in an American world that is shown in beautifully precise detail, a world of country farmhouses and county court houses and small-town hotels, of pool halls and slum apartments and the "foul, fox-smelling lairs" of cheap rooming houses, of places at Burden's Landing and the Governor's mansion and the state capital, of country fairgrounds and city football stadiums and endless highways. Moreover, this story is told us by Jack Burden who is (among other things) a trained historian and experienced newspaper man and can give us an authoritative account of the immediate meaning of the events, the tangled train of intentions and acts that cause them and flow from them. The world appears overwhelmingly real in *All the King's Men.* It is there. Because there is where experience, which is the life of the soul, occurs.

It is the wisdom of reason in looking beyond itself to experience that Jack Burden refuses—or is unable—to recognize until the very end, when he finally sees that, if knowledge is indeed the end of man as he has always believed, "all knowledge that is worth anything is maybe paid for by blood." Until then he cannot commit his soul to experience because he cannot face what experience will do to the perfection of the story his reason has made up about life. He struggles to keep his existence a timeless preserve of images of Anne Stanton afloat on the water with her eyes closed (but even then the sky was dark greenish-purple with a coming storm) and of ideas about the world that make it unreal.

> I had got hold of [a] principle out of a book when I was in college, and I had hung onto it for grim death. I owed my success in life to that principle. It had put me where I was. What you don't know won't hurt you, for it ain't real.

They called that Idealism in my book I had when I was in college, and after I got hold of that principle I became an Idealist. I was a brass-bound Idealist in those days. If you are an Idealist it does not matter what you do or what goes on around you because it isn't real anyway.

This idealism was merely Jack Burden's excuse for living as if the world of time—where people try to do their best according to their dim lights and fail and grow old—were not real. He clung to this principle "for grim death" (of the soul, at least) and secretly fancied that his failure to do anything was a special kind of success. It was a way of hiding from the knowledge of experience that "was like the second when you come home late at night and see the yellow envelope of the telegram sticking out from under your door. . . . While you stand in the hall, with the envelope in your hand, you feel there's an eye on you . . . [that] sees you huddled up way inside, in the dark which is you, inside yourself, like a clammy, sad little foetus . . . that doesn't want to know what is in that envelope. It wants to lie in the dark and not know, and be warm in its not-knowing." (When Byram White's corruption is exposed he stands before Willie Stark "drawing himself into a hunch as though he wanted to assume the prenatal position and be little and warm and safe in the dark.") Jack Burden wanted to remain forever kissing Anne Stanton in the underwater world into which she took the highest dive of her life (but when they came to the surface she swam straight for the beach). He looked longingly at the May foliage of the trees and thought of himself "inside that hollow inner chamber, in the aqueous green light, inside the great globe of the tree . . . and no chance of seeing anything . . . and no sound except, way off, the faint mumble of traffic, like the ocean chewing its gums." (This lotus-eater's dream was interrupted by Sadie Burke, who told Jack Burden that Anne Stanton had become Willie Stark's mistress.)

Jack's idealism allows him to reject as absurd caricatures of humanity the beings who fall below his standards, but it also costs him his capacity to feel, so that it is really he who does not exist humanly rather than the imperfect creatures he rejects. Anne Stanton understands this without being able to explain it.

"Oh, you just think you are sorry. Or glad. You aren't really."

"If you think you are sorry, who in hell can tell you that

you aren't?" I demanded, for I was a brass-bound Idealist then, as I have stated, and was not about to call for a plebiscite on whether I was sorry or not. . . .

"Oh, Jack," she said, ". . . can't you love them a little, or forgive them, or just not think about them, or something?"

Yet he can maintain this attitude only by an effort of self-persuasion. He has to keep telling himself that his mother is maddeningly stupid, because he is touched by the bravery of her defiance of age and wants to respond to her love when she smiles at him "with a sudden and innocent happiness, like a girl"; he dwells on the ludicrous horror of Tiny Duffy and the Boys, only to find in the end that he cannot hate even Tiny. What is worse, he is often driven perilously close to recognizing that what makes him think others subhuman exists in himself. He will not touch Anne Stanton; if he does Anne will cease to be the sleeping beauty of heart-breaking innocence he has wanted her to remain ever since he saw her floating with her eyes closed that day. Instead he marries Lois who, he imagines, is merely a "beautiful, juicy, soft, vibrant, sweet-smelling, sweet-breathed machine for provoking and satisfying the appetite." But Lois "could talk, and when something talks you sooner or later begin to listen to the sound it makes and begin, even in the face of all the other evidence, to regard it as a person . . . and the human element infects your innocent Eden pleasure in the juicy, sweet-breathed machine." When Lois thus turns out to be—honestly and stubbornly—a kind of person intolerable to anyone of even moderate standards, Jack runs away, first into the Great Sleep and then to divorce. Whenever Jack Burden is faced with the dualism of flesh and spirit he runs away. His worst moment is caused by Anne Stanton's affair with Willie Stark, when he has to flee all the way to California and discover an entirely new principle, the Great Twitch, to hide behind.

Just as Jack will not go into the world of experience with Anne Stanton, so he will not give his ideals of personal conduct the reality of action. As long as he can convince himself that he is merely a technician, he can feel he is not responsible for what is done: he is just obeying orders. When he cannot—as when he is asked to put some real feeling into his column for the *Chronicle*—he quits. When he investigates Judge Irwin for Willie Stark, he is just exercising his technique. He had tried that once before, as a Ph.D. student, when he investigated Cass Mastern. But he laid that job aside unfinished because he wanted to keep his belief that "the world was simply an accumulation of items, odds and ends of things like broken and misused and dust-shrouded things gathered in a garret," whereas Cass Mastern had "learned that the world is all of one piece . . . that the world is like an enormous spider web and if you touch it, however lightly, at any point, the vibration ripples to the remotest perimeter." Perhaps, the narrator adds, the Jack Burden of those days "laid aside the journal of Cass Mastern not because he could not understand, but because he was afraid to understand for what might be understood there was a reproach to him."

With Judge Irwin he is again the researcher, with the research man's faith that the past is only a story, that "all times are one time, and all those dead in the past never lived before our definition gives them life, and out of the shadow their eyes implore us. That is what all us historical researchers believe. And we love truth." He does his job on Judge Irwin well: "It was a perfect research job, marred in its technical perfection by only one thing: it meant something." It had been easy to drop Cass Mastern when there arose a danger that the research job would be marred by meaning. Though Cass Mastern had lived in time, it was not Jack Burden's time and it was easy to think of Cass as part of history, "the *done*." But Judge Irwin is still alive and Jack loves him, and in digging up his past Jack has brushed the spider web. He tries not to know that, but cannot escape when his mother says, "You killed him; you killed him. . . . Your father, your father and oh! you killed him."

He has had his bad moments before, as when he caught himself defending what Willie Stark had done against the sincerely selfish business men at Judge Irwin's dinner party ("the bluff, burly type, with lots of money and a manly candor"). He hastened to absolve himself of responsibility ("I didn't say I felt any way," he insisted, "I just offered a proposition for the sake of argument"), but he had come very close to understanding the possibility that—as Cass Mastern puts it—"only a man like my brother Gilbert [or Willie Stark] can in the midst of evil retain enough innocence and enough strength to . . . do a little justice in terms of the great injustice." Jack Burden does not want to understand that; he wants to go on thinking that "politics is action and all action is but a flaw in the perfection of inaction, which is peace," wants to go on not knowing that his refusal to possess Anne Stanton "had almost as dire consequences as

Cass Mastern's sin" with Annabelle Trice, his friend's wife, and far more dire consequences than the sin of his father, Judge Irwin, with the wife of Judge Irwin's friend Ellis Burden.

The real reason Jack Burden works for Willie Stark, just as it is the real reason Adam Stanton does, is the fascination for him of *doing* good, not just imagining it. But he does not want to recognize that to do good he must involve himself in the world where power is acquired, not without dust and heat, and what you do has all sorts of unexpected consequences for which you must take responsibility. So Jack Burden has to persuade himself that he is just Willie Stark's research man. It is not until Willie is dead and Jack discovers the part Tiny Duffy played in killing him that Jack considers acting on his own. Then he comes very close to telling Sugar-Boy about Tiny. He knows that will make Sugar-Boy shoot Tiny, exactly as Tiny had known that telling Adam Stanton about Anne and Willie had made Adam shoot Willie.

But Jack does not tell Sugar-Boy. Before he gets a chance to, he has gone to see Tiny and given himself the unearned pleasure of setting Tiny straight. Then Sadie Burke writes him that it would be foolish to expose Duffy "just because you got some high-falutin idea you are an Eagle Scout and [Anne Stanton] is Joan of Arc." That is the truth, and it makes him think of his own responsibility for Willie's death, and suddenly he feels himself caught in a "monstrous conspiracy whose meaning I could not fathom. . . . It was as though in the midst of the scene [with Tiny Duffy he] had slowly and like a brother winked at me with his oyster eye and I had known he knew the nightmare truth, which was that we were twins bound together more intimately and disastrously than the poor freaks of the midway who are bond by the common stitch of flesh and gristle and the seepage of blood. We were bound together forever and I could never hate him without hating myself or love myself without loving him."

That is the moment at which Jack Burden faces the truth. But until it arrives, he is a brass-bound idealist filled with something like despair by the insignificance of the existence he has been so careful to persuade himself is the only reasonable one, so that when Anne Stanton says to him, "You are such a smart aleck. . . . Aren't you ever going to grow up?" he says, "I reckon I am a smart aleck, but it is just a way to pass the time." But it does not even do that, for he wakes each morning to look out the window and see "that it [is] going to be another day" in the endless series of insignificant tomorrows. Or he watches from a train window a woman empty a pan of water and go back into her house—"To what was in the house. The floor of the house is thin against the bare ground and the walls and roof are thin against all of everything which is outside, but you cannot see through the walls to the secret to which the woman has gone in. . . . And all at once you feel like crying." For "the soul's life is experience, a given thing . . . to be known only in living." That is what makes Willie Stark so fascinating.

Willie Stark has a gift for acting in the world. As a country boy he had studied law and history with the passionate intensity of one who instinctively feels that knowledge is not so much a means of understanding as an instrument of power. "Gee," he says later with amiable contempt, "back in those days I figured those fellows knew all there was to know and I figured I was going to get me a chunk of it." What he knows by then is that you can use certain kinds of knowledge to make men do what you wish, but that is quite another thing. "No," he says to Hugh Miller, "I'm not a lawyer. I know some law. In fact, I know a lot of law. And I made me some money out of law. But I'm not a lawyer."

He began his political career with a farm boy's naïveté by trying to get the Mason City school honestly built. When the courthouse crowd kicked him out, he ran against them on his own. But nobody listened to his story about the school and he was badly beaten. His wife Lucy, who lives to remind him of the values power exists to serve—as Anne Stanton lives to remind Jack Burden of the power values exist to direct—reminds Willie that he did not want to be elected to a government of crooks anyway. But all Willie can remember is that the courthouse crowd had "run it over me. Like I was dirt," because they had the power. Then, with the collapse of the school's fire escape, Willie becomes a hero and it almost seems as if not mixing with crooks is the way to achieve power as well as virtue, for in no time there is the city politician, Tiny Duffy, on his doorstep asking him to run for governor. He never suspects Tiny is merely looking for a way to split the opponent's vote. "For the voice of Tiny Duffy summoning him was nothing but the echo of a certainty and a blind compulsion in him."

Willie sets out to campaign for governor with his earnest, boring, true speech, and Jack Burden and Sadie Burke watch him, full of the easy cynicism of the irresponsible wise. Yet they are reluctantly impressed by Willie. "You know," Sadie says one evening, " . . .

even if he found out he was a sucker, I believe he might keep right on." "Yeah," Jack says, "making those speeches." "God," she said, "aren't they awful?" "Yeah." "But I believe he might keep right on," she said. "Yeah." "The sap," she said. When Sadie turns out to be right, they both yield to the fascination of Willie's gift for action. Sadie gives herself wholly to Willie, enduring his trivial infidelities but reacting fiercely to the real betrayal of his affair with Anne Stanton, only to discover in the end that she has helped to kill the man who, whatever he had done, she could not live without.

Willie does keep on; but not making those awful speeches. The discovery that he is once more being run over like dirt strengthens his feeling that power is all that matters, and slowly, even unconsciously, he drifts away from Lucy's understanding of the values power exists for. We watch him—as he talks to Hugh Miller, to Judge Irwin, to Adam Stanton—developing his theory that the law and the good are things men of power make up as they go along until he is—in fact if not wholly in intention—merely a virtuoso of power, half believing that, by its mere exercise, men can give power a purpose, as Jack Burden, his counterpart, is merely a virtuoso of speculation, half believing that by contemplating an ideal men can change the world. When Willie reaches this point, Lucy refuses to live with him any more. But when their son, Tom, is paralyzed for life and Willie, like some pitiful Faustus, cries out that he will name his magnificent new hospital after Tom, she is there as always to remind him that "these things don't matter. Having somebody's name cut on a piece of stone. Getting it in the papers. All those things. Oh, Willie, he was my baby boy, he was our baby boy, and those things don't matter, they don't ever matter, don't you see?"

There is something in Willie that always recognizes that, too, even when he is exercising his political skill with the least regard for it. When his cunning but unscrupulous maneuver to save Byram White leads Hugh Miller to resign, he says to Miller in semi-comic woe, "You're leaving me all alone with the sons-of-bitches. Mine and the other fellow's"; and when he blackmails the legislature into voting down his impeachment, he says to Jack Burden that Lincoln seems to have been wrong when he said a house divided against itself cannot stand, since the government he presides over "is sure half slave and half son-of-a-bitch, and it is standing." When he begins to plan his great free hospital, he refuses to allow it to be built in the usual crooked way. He is not just remembering the collapse of the

Mason City school's fire escape; he can prevent Gummy Larsen from building shoddily even if Gummy does take a cut of the school contract. What he is remembering is what made him want that school built honestly. This insistence that the hospital be built without graft is, as Jack Burden says, "scarcely consistent" with Willie's constant assertions that you always have to make good out of bad, but it maddens him that Jack Burden—who has not yet learned to look beyond reason—cannot understand why, just after Willie has saved Byram White from his deserved punishment, he wants to build that hospital with clean hands.

Thus, in the confrontation of its two central characters, *All the King's Men* poses what is for Mr. Warren the central problem of existence, the irrepressible conflict between the conception of life that gives action meaning and value and the act of living in the world in which meaning and value have to be realized. This conflict appears unendurable. Yet both Jack Burden, who tries to exist in the conception without accepting the responsibility of action, and Willie Stark, who drifts into acting effectively for its own sake, find it impossible not to know that it must be endured.

"This," as Jack says near the end of the novel, "has been the story of Willie Stark, but it is my story, too." As Willie, living the practical life of power, is haunted by a desire to use his power in a virtuous way he denies is possible, so Jack Burden, prevented from acting by his concern for the virtue he can imagine, is haunted by a desire to realize himself in the world he denies is real. This is the story the novel tells about Jack Burden. But the novel is Jack Burden's story in another sense: he tells it. It was a risk to use as narrator a central character whose changing conception of the nature of experience is the main issue in the novel. It is like making Emma Woodhouse, Lambert Strether, and Lord Jim the narrators of their novels. If it could be brought off, the meaning of the action could be revealed dramatically, from within and behind the view of a character who is limited by his own nature and does not understand that meaning for a long time; and when this meaning finally emerges on the surface of the novel, it will be the product of an experience that has been fully represented in the novel and will not be arbitrarily given, as is, for example, Marlow's view of life in Conrad's *Lord Jim*. But it is very difficult to keep separate the limited view of the events a character has as he is living through them and the view he finally takes, when the events are all over and he sits down to write the story. Mr. Warren brings off this difficult maneuver, and it is well worth what it costs. But that cost is nonetheless the considerable one of making the novel very easy to misunderstand.

The voice of Jack Burden conveys three distinct feelings about the events he describes. It is, most obviously, the voice of Jack Burden the idealist who sardonically points out the plentiful evidence that life is grotesquely absurd. He does that very effectively and what he shows us is hard to deny. At the same time the tone of his voice is almost hysterically extravagant. That extravagance gives a hectic rhetorical brilliance to his descriptions of the world's absurdities, but why should he care that much if the world is beneath contempt? His extravagance is really the expression of the second of Jack Burden's feelings, his longing to reach beyond reason to the secret of experience that he is debarred from by the refusal of Jack Burden the Idealist to believe experience is real.

The idealist's rhetoric always belittles the world by contrasting the indignity of its shoddy physical nature with some dignified image of the soul.

> I'd be lying there in the hole in the middle of my bed where the springs had given down with the weight of wayfaring humanity, lying there on my back with my clothes on and looking up at the ceiling and watching the cigarette smoke flow up slowly and splash against the ceiling . . . like the pale uncertain spirit rising up out of your mouth on the last exhalation, the way the Egyptians figured it, to leave the horizontal tenement of clay in its ill-fitting pants and vest.

How silly to describe men in grand terms when they are all what Jack says Lois's friends are: "There was nothing particularly wrong with them. They were just the ordinary garden variety of human garbage"—whose "wayfaring" produces nothing but broken springs in cheap-hotel bedrooms, whose "pale, uncertain spirit" is only cigarette smoke, whose "tenement of clay" is dressed in ill-fitting pants and vest.

The idealist Jack Burden is, then, always saying, "Go to, I'll no more on't." But just the same "it hath made [him] mad," or nearly so, and like Hamlet, once he is launched on a description of it, he cannot stop torturing himself ("Nay but to live / In the rank sweat of an enseamed bed, / Stewed in corruption"); until slowly, as we listen, we begin to feel, not that men's lives are less horrible than he says they are, but that there is some imperfectly fulfilled intention in them not unlike Jack Burden's own—some dim light—that makes them pitiful rather than disgusting. Consider, for example, Mortimer Lonzo Littlepaugh who was fired by the American Electric Power Company in order that Judge Irwin might be paid off with his job "at a salary they never paid me." Mortimer is almost as absurd as his name, and his indignation is a fantastic mixture of "confusion, weakness, piety, self-pity, small-time sharpness, vindictiveness." "I gave them my heart's blood," he writes his sister just before he commits suicide, "all these years. And they call him vice-president, too. They lied to me and they cheated me and they make him vice-president for taking a bribe. . . . I am going to join our sainted Mother and Father who were kind and good . . . and will greet me on the Other Shore, and dry every tear. . . . P. S. If they [the insurance company] know I have done what I am going to do they will not pay you." "So," as Jack Burden observes, "the poor bastard had gone to the Other Shore, where Mother and Father would dry away every tear, immediately after having instructed his sister how to defraud the insurance company"—to no purpose, he might have added, since Mortimer had borrowed practically the full value of his insurance. Mortimer Lonzo Littlepaugh was certainly grotesque, but with a passionate sincerity that is, however absurd, also pitiful.

The same double response is evoked by the tone of the narrator's voice as he describes the characteristic life of his time. "A funeral parlor at midnight is ear-splitting," he will say about a cheap joint, "compared to the effect you get in the middle of the morning in the back room of a place like Slades. . . . You sit there and think how cozy it was last night, with the effluvium of brotherly bodies and the haw-haw of camaraderie, and you look at the floor . . . and the general impression is that you are alone with the Alone and it is His move." Or, driving past the comically tasteless and pitifully decaying Victorian houses of Mason City, he will notice "the sad valentine lace of gingerbread work around the veranda"; or he will observe the absurd and touching awe of the girl in Doc's drugstore who, seeing Willie Stark standing there at the counter, "got a look on her face as though her garter belt had busted in church." People are certainly ridiculous—vain, pretentious, foolish—as Jack Burden, who is being a smart aleck to pass the time, can see very clearly; they are also pitiful—sincere, eager, committed—as another Jack Burden cannot help feeling.

The third and most important feeling Jack Burden's voice expresses is the feeling that ultimately resolves the conflict between these two, the feeling of the Jack Burden who is telling us this story. This Jack Burden seldom speaks to us directly, and when he does it is mainly to remind us that what Jack Burden felt when he was living through these events was different from what he feels now, as he tells about them. "If I learned anything from studying history," he will say, "that was what I learned. Or, to be more exact, that was what I thought I had learned." Or he will say, "at least that is how I argued the case then"; but he does not say how he argues it now.

Only at the end of the novel do we learn that, discover that Jack Burden, without ceasing to believe in the reality of man's reason, has come to believe also in the reality of experience. Life, he now knows, is not "only a story" in the timelessness of which "the *done*" and "the *to-be-done*" are one. But if he now knows that "the *being done*" exists beyond any story man's reason invents about it, he also knows that story represents man's idea of it and determines the way he will act in it. The very existence of *All the King's Men* demonstrates that, for the controlling element in the narrator's voice is not Jack Burden the idealist or Jack Burden the historian but the Jack Burden who has come to understand that "the soul's life is experience," and thus believes, "in my way," what Ellis Burden says as he is dying, that "the creation of evil is . . . the index of God's glory and His power. That had to be so that the creation of good might be the index of man's glory and his power. But by God's help. By His help and in His wisdom."

We sometimes hear the man who knows that in the way the narrator puzzles over an ostensibly virtuous act, as when he says of Jack Burden's conduct that night in his bedroom at Burden's Landing that Anne Stanton "trusted me, but perhaps for that moment of hesitation I did not trust myself, and looked back upon the past as something precious about to be snatched away from us and was afraid of the future. . . . Then there came the day when that image was taken from me. I learned that Anne Stanton had become the mistress of Willie Stark, that somehow by an obscure and necessary logic I had handed her over to him." Sometimes we hear it in an ostensibly accidental observation, as when he notes that "later on love vines will climb up, out of the weeds," around the sign of the skull and crossbones put up where people have died on the highway. Jack Burden does not notice that because it is a relevant to his sardonic description of life in the age of the internal combustion engine; it is the image of some larger meaning of experience.

This larger meaning is in fact present behind everything he tells us, as it is behind the whole description of that drive up route 58 with which the novel begins. There is Sugar-Boy taking every risk he can in order to exercise his uncanny skill as a driver and satisfy his naïve need to act effectively in the world by slipping between truck and hay wagon with split-second timing ("The b-b-b-b-bas-tud—he seen me c-c-c-c-com-ing"). There is Willie Stark enjoying every minute of this dangerous game. There is Jack Burden thinking it was a pleasure to watch if you could forget it was real, but not willing to know, as Willie Stark does, that only if it is real does it have what Cass Mastern calls "the kind of glory, however stained or obscured, [that is] in whatever man's hand does well."

That drive was a wholly natural event, the politician being driven at politician's speed to his home town to get himself photographed at his pappy's farm for the newspapers. But it sets Jack Burden brooding about the age of the internal combustion engine and the cars whirling along the new slab Willie had built for them, the boys imagining themselves Barney Oldfields and the girls wearing no panties "on account of the climate" and their knees apart "for the cool." It is an absurd way for the human beings to behave; and yet Jack Burden knows too that "the smell of gasoline and burning brake bands and red-eye is sweeter than myrrh" and that the girls "have smooth little faces to break your heart." It is all very like the life of man, which moves through time at a breakneck clip that some enjoy too much and some are too frightened by but which is the unavoidable condition. It is far more dangerous than the gay ones suspect, for the sheer speed of it can easily hypnotize you and "you'll come to just at the moment when the right front wheel hooks over into the black dirt off the slab, and you'll try to jerk her back on. . . . But you won't make it of course." Probably not; but, as the frightened ones refuse to admit, you have to risk it if you are ever to smell the frankincense and myrrh.

In this way the whole story of *All the King's Men* becomes a kind of metaphor. The events of the novel are the incidents of a journey every man takes up that highway toward the River of Death (if not so surely to any Celestial City beyond it). For each wayfarer the other characters represent different ideas of how to get there as incomplete and partial as his own is for them. Each of Willie Stark's women, for example, represents a mode of travel he adopts for a time. Lucy, the school teacher, has the country people's simple notion of virtue and lives by it with unfailing integrity, leaving Willie when he discovers he cannot hold onto it and gain power; but Lucy has to go right on believing that Willie, whom she had loved and married and borne a son to, is, with all his faults, a great man. When Willie discovers how to gain power, he takes up with Sadie Burke who, having fought her way up from the bitter poverty of her childhood, plays the game of power with fierce determination; and when Willie takes Anne Stanton as his mistress and Jack Burden, seeing Sadie's suffering, says characteristically, "If it's all that grief, let him go," she says, "Let him go! let him go! I'll kill him first, I swear"— and does. Willie makes Anne Stanton his mistress when he discovers in himself a need not just for power but to do good with clean hands. Anne Stanton has shared something of her brother Adam's dream of an ideal past in which those who governed were heroic figures; she has always known it is not enough, but it makes her able to give those who, like Willie, govern now a sense of greatness. Anne comes to love Willie when she learns that he, whom she had supposed a wholly wicked man because he was not perfectly good, has done much good—"Does he mean that, Jack? Really?"—and that her father, whom she had supposed perfectly good, had done evil. Each of these women is for Willie Stark the embodiment of the idea he lives by while he loves her, as Willie is for each of them. So each character is for all the others he knows.

Through most of the novel, Jack Burden is suspended between Adam Stanton, the friend of his youth, and Willie Stark, the friend of his maturity, and between Ellis Burden, the father who had loved to make the child Jack Burden happy and lived only to care for the helpless children of the world after he learned that his wife had become the mistress of his best friend, and, Judge Irwin, the father who did not scare but loved Jack's mother and took her, was an upright judge all his life except once, when he was desperate, and taught Jack to shoot ("You got to lead a duck, son").

For Jack, Adam Stanton is the romantic who "has a picture of the world in his head, and when the world doesn't conform in any respect to that picture, he wants to throw the world away. Even if it means throwing out the baby with the bath. Which . . . it always does mean." Jack ought to know; it is what he did when he refused to touch Anne Stanton. Adam Stanton refuses to believe people need anything but justice. But Willie Stark who, like Judge Irwin, has the courage to act what he feels, is one of the people and knows that "Your need is my justice." Jack Burden is, to start with, too like Adam Stanton to believe that the grotesque world he lives in can be put together again, even by all the king's men, and for a long time he refuses to touch it. But in the end he is too much like Willie Stark not to understand Willie's dying words—"It might have been all different, Jack. You got to believe that"—and to know he must try. As the novel ends, he has married Anne Stanton and is living with her in Judge Irwin's house, that relatively permanent—and lifeless—expression of the values handed down to him from the past, writing the history of Willie Stark's life. But he and Anne are about to leave that house and the writing of history and to enter the process of history, the life of their times. "And soon now," as Jack says in the novel's last sentence, "we shall go out of the house and go into the convulsion of the world, out of history into history and the awful responsibility of Time."

Robert Penn Warren
as a Philosophical Novelist

Allen Shepherd

Of recent years much of the critical discussion of the fiction of Robert Penn Warren has been characterized by a rather striking polarity of perspective. Thus in a not untypical conjunction one finds in the spring, 1968, issue of *The Southern Review,* Walter Sullivan virtually dismissing all of Warren's work published since 1946, and John Rees Moore accurately anatomizing a volume of critical essays as a loyalist counterattack against the perversely unenlightened. Although the distinction is not absolute, many of those who do Warren reverence or tender their respects devote their attention to Warren the man of ideas, the philosophical novelist, while those who are not impressed or who look with narrowed eye on the falling star, often imply that Warren is not properly serious, and that he is to be regarded as an entertainer, a popular novelist. That the popular and the serious should commonly be treated as antithetical is but one indication of the prejudicial nature of much contemporary American literary criticism. Warren is neither a philosophical nor a popular novelist; he is both—and when in good form, as he usually is, both simultaneously.

Whatever else may be said of him, Warren is not—in the usual sense of the word—a philosopher, certainly not a systematic philosopher. He may well, however, be called a philosophical novelist, a term for which Warren has himself provided an apposite definition in his essay on Conrad's *Nostromo.* There we read that

---

From *Western Humanities Review* 24, no. 2 (Spring 1970). © 1970 by the University of Utah.

> The philosophical novelist, or poet, is one for whom the documentation of the world is constantly striving to rise to the level of generalization about values, for whom the image strives to rise to symbol, for whom images always fall into a dialectical configuration, for whom the urgency of experience, no matter how vividly and strongly experience may enchant, is the urgency to know the meaning of experience. This is not to say the philosophical novelist is schematic and deductive. It is to say quite the contrary, that he is willing to go naked into the pit, again and again, to make the same old struggle for his truth.

Nowhere could one find a more succinct statement of Warren's aims and methods in fiction nor a more suggestive intimation of his strengths and limitations. Although Warren has never published a novel that offers only "documentation of the world," however expert and compelling, neither has he—with one notable exception—failed to create a vital and concrete narrative. The strength of his most successful novels, of *All the King's Men* for example, derives in good measure from the organic union of "documentation" and "generalization about values," from the unforced evolution of the general and abstract from the particular and concrete. Those of his novels which are less successful, *Wilderness* for example, fail in part because generalization parallels but seldom touches documentation. The "image [which] strives to rise to symbol" offers a refinement of the previously stated attempt, as the limited sensory experience takes on a more inclusive significance. That "dialectical configuration" in which the images align themselves is indicative of logical, systematic thought, moral discrimination and consequent polarization. "Experience," with its potent and seemingly almost malign influence, recalls the "documentation" with which the definition begins, and—as before—the philosophical novelist's aim is said to be to extract from that precious and magnetic element a core of meaning, while in the process doing no violence to the unrefined substance. To say, as Warren next does, that the philosophical novelist is not "schematic and deductive" is to assert a right relation between experience and the meaning of experience. The final naked plunge of the novelist into the pit represents not so much an unarmed descent into the self as a return to the seductive realm of turbulent and undifferentiated experience. The effort expended by the novelist is directed to three objectives: to resist the lure of unordered and hence ungraspable experience, to analyze while still preserving intact that experience, and to resolve or accept the antinomies which reflection reveals.

Warren's definition of the philosophical novelist does not of course identify his own ideas, but it does suggest both their primacy in his fiction and something of the way in which they are organized and presented. It should be said that Warren is not a notably original thinker, not a seminal intellect. He has not, as a novelist, been trailed by a school, by an identifiable body of followers, as has William Faulkner. Warren seems to have come to many of his principal themes by the time he was thirty-five, or—to fix upon a convenient date— by 1939, the year in which he published his first novel, *Night Rider*. It is sometimes observed that Warren is an unusually consistent thinker, and this is an accurate characterization, so long as it does not imply mere repetition or elaboration. What is noteworthy and what makes reading Warren a continuing pleasure is one's developing sense of the evolution, refinement, and testing of ideas in new contexts, of chances taken, new possibilities envisaged, new approaches to truth undertaken.

Warren's most outspoken statement of his primary ideas is an essay entitled "Knowledge and the Image of Man," published in 1955. "The story of every soul," he says on the first page, "is the story of its self-definition for good or evil, salvation or damnation." This being so, "we are committed to recognize the right of every soul to that knowledge necessary for its best fulfillment." The ulti- mate significance of the self is to be discovered in the world through what Warren terms "an inevitable osmosis of being," by means of which "man creates new perspectives, discovers new values—that is, a new self—and so the identity is continually emerging, an unfold- ing, a self-affirming and, we hope, a self-corrective creation." The end of self-fulfillment is wholeness of spirit, achieved in unity with man and nature. Meaningful self-fulfillment, however, presupposes separateness, in which state man, if he is fortunate, discovers the pain of self-criticism, which may lead him to develop a depersonalized ideal of excellence. This ideal established, "he may achieve the cour- age and clarity of mind to envisage the tragic pathos of life, and once he realizes that the tragic experience is universal and a corollary of man's place in nature, he may return to a communion with man and nature."

Central in Warren's conception of self-fulfillment in communion is the nature of what may be termed the dialogic life of the self, since the fundamental conflict of his novels is personal before it is social. This dialogic life has three dimensions: with self, with others, and with some superhuman principle. Most often Warren concerns himself with the first and second dimensions, and his characters discover that however great or however conscious one's effort, the mystery of other selves can never be fully penetrated, which is to say that man's knowledge of others is both precious and fitful, that the epiphany comes but seldom. So it is with most of Warren's lovers, married couples, brothers and sisters, male comrades. The self nonetheless sees other selves as an instrument for its purposes and as completion for its incompleteness. Thus the search for knowledge may and often does result in the attempted exploitation of others. Such exploitation seems almost generic in Warren's protagonists. The efforts of Amantha Starr in *Band of Angels* are more intense and protracted than most, but in her struggles are clearly represented both the desire for and the resistance to such knowledge. Yet the self cannot be truly fulfilled unless it is drawn out of itself into the life of another. Essays at this fulfillment are often suggested in sexual relations, as is notably the case in *The Cave*. Most importantly, there must be an element of reverence or of reservation in even the most mutual relation, which indicates the sin of those who callously draw their sustenance from others, as do Bogan Murdock and Slim Sarrett in *At Heaven's Gate*. While it is the unique center of life, the individual self is, through memory and imagination, indeterminately open to other selves. This idea informs the strategy of many of Warren's retrospective short stories, such as "Blackberry Winter," and suggests the desired effect of the historical novels, such as *Band of Angels,* as well as of the Cass Mastern episode in *All the King's Men*. Since the pattern of all these dialogues is conditioned by historic factors, one can appreciate a central motive for Warren's painstaking construction of Kentucky in the 1820s (*World Enough and Time*) or New Orleans in the 1860s (*Band of Angels*).

Both the dialogue of the self with itself and that of the self with other selves point beyond themselves to the third dimension, the dialogue of the self with the supernatural, and it is this dimension, beyond those of communion with man and nature, which Warren often treats rather obliquely but does not define. So one is to understand the tentativeness of the resolutions of most of his novels: of Jack Burden's in *All the King's Men,* of Jeremiah Beaumont's in *World*

Enough and Time, of Adam Rosenzweig's in *Wilderness,* in all of which the hero achieves a communion whose transcendental nature is only suggested. The one certain measure of their success, however, is that they have pressed beyond the first dimension, that they have given over the idolatrous and essentially romantic attempt to establish the ultimate significance of the self.

The acquiring of that knowledge necessary for self-fulfillment entails the attempt to grasp or perhaps even to resolve the contradictions or polarities which seem to define man's experience of the world. It is usually a character's perception of these polarities, and the resulting sense of shock and imbalance, that leads or drives him to a redefinition of his experience which will comprehend apparent contradictions.

Man finds himself to be a creature of nature, but must in his effort to define himself as human assert his differences, moral and ethical, from nature, must not descend into brute existence. A related error is that which leads man to a violation of nature, either in ignoring it, or in exploiting it, or in reducing it to an abstraction. Of the first error, Jeremiah Beaumont provides an example; of the second, Bogan Murdock. The process of self-definition entails a resolution, usually provisional, of the efficacy of man's will and of its relation to deity or natural law. Man yearns for justice, but is governed, sometimes even executed, by the law which he can make and break, and which is thus subject to all manner of human frailties. Yet the man who attempts to strike through the law for his justice, as does Percy Munn of *Night Rider,* falls into monomania or demagoguery. The defined self comprehends in dynamic balance idea and action; seeking definition in idea (Beaumont), or in action (Munn) leads to that imbalance which issues in fanaticism. It is usually the case that such desperate single-mindedness will manifest itself first in one sort of imbalance and then in the other. So it is with both Munn and Beaumont.

The idea or ideal, for its validity to be determined, must be tested and shaped in action, in the world. Often, as in *All the King's Men,* the real and the ideal, here the pragmatist (the "real" intensified), Willie Stark, and the idealist (the idea intensified), Adam Stanton, are in their mutual incompleteness drawn to and destructive of one another. And although there may be in the private world a reservoir of socially viable values, the man who withdraws, literally or figuratively, into himself, is prone to that self-idolatry which negates even the possibility of self-fulfilling communion. The achievement of self-fulfillment involves struggle, with self and with others: the process is dynamic. Retreat from the world is a denial of the possibility of redemption through knowledge, it is the acceptance of fatal stasis. Such a withdrawal tempts most of Warren's central characters, notably Jack Burden. The assertion of innocence is the assertion of noninvolvement, it is the attempt not to transcend but to escape one's humanity. The acceptance of guilt does not suggest so much the admission of the discreditable motivation of certain of one's overt acts as the acknowledgement of one's radical imperfection, shared with and uniting one with one's fellow man. Again, few of Warren's protagonists are immune to the seductive or narcotic powers of self-proclaimed innocence. Amantha Starr, of *Band of Angels,* provides a representative example.

That communion with man and nature which is the end of self-fulfillment presupposes an isolation which is tantamount to alienation, but which may prove therapeutic, may, that is, make for a union in which the defined self exists consubstantially with man and with nature. A period of therapeutic isolation followed by a renewal of communion is illustrated in the career of Yasha Jones, of *Flood.* Man as a natural creature is trapped in the finitude of time, but he may experience, though rarely, self-transcending moments when, as it seems, he knows timelessness. The promise entailed in such a revelation is as affecting as it is mysterious, and ever after the man who in an apocalyptic moment has felt himself out of time, must struggle to retain the sense of timelessness in time. One such terrifying moment is experienced by Jack Harrick in *The Cave.* Although most men are not vouchsafed such enlightenment, a number may perceive the interrelatedness of time, the interpenetration of time past and time present, and the necessity of accepting one's past as a prerequisite to a genuine future. Such perception, in some degree, is accorded most of Warren's protagonists.

A number of Warren's principal characters engage in detective work of one sort or another, rooting about for the facts. Inevitably Jack Burden, who proves himself a talented investigator, comes to mind, and indeed there emerges from *All the King's Men* a parable of fact and truth. Burden, in pursuing a Ph.D. he does not really want, gathers the facts of Cass Mastern's brief life, but the facts don't seem to make sense to him. Actually, Burden—possessed of no discernible moral orientation himself—cannot face comparison with Mastern, another young man who had devoted his life to trying to find a moral position for himself. Although the truth is not altogether lost—the dissertation manuscript is carried about from place to place—Burden is not ready to accept the truth until he has completed a second investigation, this of certain events in the early career of Judge Irwin. Burden works with practiced skill, and Irwin commits suicide. Facts, things done, may kill. Warren does not assert that facts are necessarily fatal or—alternatively—that the truth shall make you free. He does suggest that unless a man have within a moral organizing principle, the facts will profit him but little.

Some of Warren's ideas seem to have been developed by working out his criticism of certain liberal presuppositions: faith in man's reason, in his innate goodness, in moral progress in history. Warren's response to these presuppositions may in its essence be termed pragmatic, which is to say that it issued from his perception that these liberal theses do not conform to the facts of experience. The direction and purpose of Warren's critique is perhaps most evident in his treatment of Thomas Jefferson, in *Brother to Dragons,* and here the question one ought to ask is: where does Jefferson begin and where does he end? Horrified at the bestial crime of his nephew, Lilburn Lewis, who has chopped up a Negro slave, Jefferson begins in Hobbesian contempt for man, this attitude diametrically opposed to his former belief in man's natural goodness. What he eventually achieves is a fruitful reconciliation between aspiration and reality, between the disparities of experience, a mean between agonized pessimism and uncritical optimism. What he learns is that although human nature may seem monstrous, there can also transpire an enlargement of our possibilities beyond those predicated by any superficially optimistic philosophy. When Jefferson acknowledges Lewis, when he accepts his involvement or complicity in his nephew's deed, he dispels that pride inseparable from the judging of another by one's own standards, and attains the humility necessary to inner balance. Jefferson at the end of the poem is a chastened but not a disillusioned man, whose belief in man's potentialities has in fact been strengthened, who can "believe in virtue," who can affirm "the glory of the human effort."

Jefferson's, and by extension, Warren's ultimate reasoned position is thus one of qualified optimism or meliorative pessimism. Shock-induced and hence uncritical pessimism can lead either to the deadening mechanism of Jack Burden or to the near hysteria of

Jefferson. The liberal idealist, however, is always so preoccupied with his own virtues, which he gratuitously attributes to others, that he has no residual awareness of the common characteristics in all human frailties, and cannot bear to be reminded that there is a hidden kinship between the vices of even the most vicious and the virtues of even the most upright. What the idealist cannot stand, then, is the mixed nature of reality. Thus his dream of rationally ordered historic process, which founders on his ambivalent attempts as spectator or manager to find or impose reason on nature. In either case, he imagines himself to be freer than he really is: he cannot come to terms with the limits of all human striving, the fragmentariness of all human wisdom, the precariousness of all configurations of power. His attempts to determine cause and effect—a frequent preoccupation of Warren's characters—always lead him into the shadow of mystery, for his specific duties and responsibilities are undertaken within a vast web of relations whose structure he cannot penetrate. This is essentially the conclusion of Cass Mastern, of *All the King's Men*.

What Mastern, and perhaps Jack Burden, with Jeremiah Beaumont, come to realize is that nothing worth doing can be completely fulfilled in our lifetime, that nothing which is good, true, or beautiful makes complete sense in one's immediate historical context, that nothing one does, however virtuous, can be accomplished alone, and that no virtuous act of one's own seems quite as virtuous to others, friend or foe, as to oneself. To what extent such realization leads to one's being saved, respectively, by hope, faith, love, and forgiveness, it is sometimes in particular instances difficult to determine. Yet if Warren does not, as he says, "illustrate" these virtues, they are well represented in his novels. Jeremiah Beaumont dies in hope, in the hope or belief that the meaning of his life can be completed only in death: thus he goes back, to certain death, to shake the hangman's hand. Jack Burden asserts his faith that Willie Stark was a great man, that he was goodness corrupted, that—in Stark's last words—it "might have been all different." Lettice Tolliver, of *Flood*, after spending World War II as a Navy nurse, achieves fulfillment only as a lay member of an order of Roman Catholic nuns, thereby formalizing that charity which has supported her. Forgiveness is the problem of a number of Warren's characters, and one novel, *Band of Angels*, is specifically devoted to the achievement and meaning of forgiveness, to Amantha Starr's acceptance and forgiveness of her father.

The terms employed—hope, faith, love, and forgiveness—have a distinctly religious sound to them, and it might be well at this point to consider Warren as a "Christian writer," a tag sometimes attached to him. While this is not a question that can be definitively resolved, it is distinctly relevant to a consideration of Warren as a philosophical novelist. Certainly the South was in Warren's formative years, as it is today, the most conservative of all American regions in virtually all departments of life and thought. In Warren we are dealing with a writer who comes out of a traditional society, a society which has a religious substructure, in which there is much active and more residual Christianity. Warren's approach to the nature of history, one might say, accords with the biblical Christian view, which finds man's historical experience both meaningful and mysterious, and which regards the freedom of man as the source of evil as well as good. Warren seems always to have close at hand the great Christian symbols, he is engaged by the historical and doctrinal problems of Christianity, and opposes the oversimplifications of pseudo-science and scientism which are the meat and drink of what has been called a post-Christian age.

Randall Stewart, in an interesting if sometimes incautious book entitled *American Literature and Christian Doctrine,* sets up what he terms the five basic assumptions of Christian orthodoxy. They run as follows: (1) the sovereignty of God, (2) the divinity of Christ, (3) Original Sin, (4) the atonement, and (5) the inspiration of Scriptures. It may well be urged that no one would attribute to Warren the religious orthodoxy of, for example, Allen Tate. What is noteworthy, however, is the degree of contiguity between Warren's ideas and those assumptions posited by Stewart. The first assumption is implicit in virtually all of Warren's work. And as in Faulkner, there is in Warren the basic premise of original sin, conceived as a metaphor of the human condition, of radically imperfect man. There is everywhere emphasis upon the conflict between the flesh and the spirit, the necessity of discipline, man's disposition to evil, and the possibly redemptive nature of suffering. Yet the condition of man, imperfect and predestinated though it may be, is a condition of responsibility. Thus Jack Burden's last words: "we shall go out of the house and go into the convulsion of the world, out of history into history and the awful responsibility of Time." Or RPW's final address: "I opened the sagging gate, and was prepared / To go into the world of action and liability." Such observations do not themselves establish Warren as a Christian writer, yet they are relevant to a definition of his philosophical position; they do suggest that one may with some confidence place him in the biblical Christian tradition.

"The end of man," Warren says somewhere, "is to know," for that, as Willie Stark says in one of the dramatic versions of *All the King's Men,* "is the last ambition." There is a sense, then, in which Warren's primary theme, the achievement of self-fulfillment, is a variation on the fortunate fall, since many of his protagonists begin in innocence and after long travail end in comparative wisdom. Amantha Starr, Jack Burden, and Jeremiah Beaumont learn what might be called the moral turpitude of innocence, which is essentially a denial of responsibility and fallibility, the unresponsible and unethical exercise of will.

Warren has never addressed himself to specifically "religious" subjects in the manner of Graham Greene, nor has his fiction the doctrinal content of T. S. Eliot's poetry. The religious predicaments of Flannery O'Connor's characters find no close analogues in Warren's novels. While it is true that the conclusions at which Warren's characters arrive are amenable to religious interpretation, it is usually the case that they are themselves wary of any specifically religious reading of experience. So in *All the King's Men* Jack Burden offers a kind of secular transcription for Ellis Burden's unorthodox theology.

There is evident in Warren's fiction a perception that, in order to present his insights into the nature of the human condition honestly and fairly, he must take into account the climate of opinion in which he and his audience live, the fact, that is, that most of his readers are hostile or neutral to religious ideas. From this perception there seems to have developed a dual approach to ideas, religious or otherwise. One finds, usually in the poetry, the method of sometimes cryptic indirection, and in the prose, more often in recent years, the method of simple assertion. One may say, in fact, that Warren's principal temptation as a philosophical novelist has always been the inclination toward direct theorizing, although he has never written a novel of ideas in the Huxleyan sense, that is, of disembodied propositions. Warren develops his ideas in a dialectical pattern, in a system of polarities, and this structure of polarities is sometimes elevated to the level of enduring contradiction, these contradictions deriving from the amphibian nature of man, a creature of body and spirit, of necessity and freedom. What Warren's characters seek is a resolution of these contradictions, which is peculiarly difficult, since the polarities may overlap and intersect one another.

Warren's novels sometimes fail in part, it seems, for one of two reasons: because the polarities are over-elaborated or clumsily established, or because they are so convincingly stated that they resist the concluding reconciliation. *Flood* provides an instance of the first kind of failure. Bradwell Tolliver and Yasha Jones, the twin heroes of the novel, are intended to represent one of Warren's more common polarities, that of the man of fact and the man of idea. They are to work together on a motion picture, and they are to learn from one another. Warren's treatment of them, however, focuses alternately upon Bradwell's fornications and Yasha's impromptu lectures. The lectures suggest Warren's real concern with ideas, which here amounts to an imposition of thoughtfulness, the fornications his defensive attitude toward his audience. The clearest example of the second sort of failure is *Band of Angels*. Amantha Starr, Warren's protagonist, is the daughter of a white plantation owner and his Negro slave. Her half-caste status, indicative of radical internal division, for most of the novel determines her sense of herself, her every response to others. Yet apparently Warren had in mind an illustration of the achievement of wholeness, to be accomplished, one can only say, by sleight of hand. Unfortunately in this instance the hand is not faster than the eye, and one sees where the handkerchief has gone. The essential result of such a conclusion is the devaluation of the apparently well established polarity.

Warren's world view may be characterized as tragic-ironic, the emphasis in the hyphenated adjective about equally divided. Man is an ironic creature because he forgets who he is, because he denies his own identity as both creature and creator. He denies the mixed nature of reality in his unending attempt to disentangle the indefinitely extending relatedness of all he knows or can know. From good comes evil, from evil, good. Yet man's situation is tragic in that evil and destructiveness seem the almost inevitable consequences of his creativity. The great evils of history, his own and the world's, seem inherent in his pretensions, which are the result or concomitant of his freedom.

If the common pragmatic justification of religion—that without religion morality collapses—would not seem attractive to Warren, there is something in his novels of the William James of *The Varieties of Religious Experience,* that is, a belief that "religious experience" is a perfectly straightforward form of experience, with unique, and on the whole, desirable results, and that the test of the genuineness or efficacy of such experience is its capacity to transform the whole person. In all Warren's novels the test of the truthfulness of ideas is to be found in the relation between ideas and their consequences in action. Ideas are subject to continuous retesting and reshaping, since an idea which is "true" at any given time for any given person is not necessarily "true" for others or even for that same person under different circumstances. This conception of an open-ended or unfinished universe underlies Warren's attachment to provisional judgments and virtually negates the possibility of formulating a final, absolute "truth." Absolute truth or absolute knowledge is clearly not what Warren's work springs from or pretends to achieve. Nor is his fiction based on a formal program or a fully articulated criticism of society. It springs rather from a need, both intellectual and emotional, to confront the incoherencies and paradoxes of life, to face the divisive polarities of the self. The confrontation is dynamic, continuing, and the resolutions achieved always inchoate. While one might easily overstate the case, it appears that Warren's is at least compatible with Jamesian psychology, particularly with that reconciliation of heredity and biology with effort and choice, that is, of determinism and free will, expressed in *Principles of Psychology*.

Warren is commonly associated with three now celebrated groups or schools, the Fugitives, the Agrarians, and the New Critics. Estimating their influence on Warren's mature thought as it is embodied in his novels is the more involved because of internal dissent and shifting allegiances within these groups and because of the evolutionary development of Fugitive to Agrarian, Agrarian to New Critic. This line of descent has been intensely scrutinized of recent years, and my observations will consequently be summary in nature.

Warren was twenty-one when *The Fugitive* suspended publication in 1926. When in 1957 he told an interviewer that "in a very important way, that group [the Fugitives] was my education," he was talking about his introduction to "individual writers, poems, and books through them," about a common concern with "techniques regarded as means of expression," about the "feeling that poetry was a vital activity, . . . related to ideas and to life," about a "sense of how literature can be related to place and history." Although, as he recalled, "there was little or no talk in those days about fiction," Warren seems clearly to have imbibed the principles enunciated in a statement of Fugitive policy: rejection of the romanticism, parochialism, superficiality, and sentimentalism of the then dominant southern cultural tradition.

Among the twelve Southerners who contributed to *I'll Take My Stand* (1930), the preeminent thinkers were John Crowe Ransom, Allen Tate and Donald Davidson. Warren, then twenty-five, offered "The Briar Patch," whose moderate segregationist views he has since grown away from, as is evident in his novels, in *Segregation: The Inner Conflict in the South* (1956), in the *Paris Review* interview of 1957, and in *Who Speaks for the Negro?* (1965). Warren's contribution to *Who Owns America: A New Declaration of Independence* (1936), "Literature as a Symptom," is in effect a plea for, or a defense of, regionalism in literature, whose strength, he asserts, derives from its apprehension and evocation of the past, of traditional values, and from its attachment to the land and the people living on it. If Warren would still maintain some of the principles of the Agrarians, particularly the dehumanizing effect of collectivism, industrialism, metropolitanism, and finance capitalism, his interests, like those of most of the Agrarians, have in good part shifted away from the sociological and the economic to the literary.

Among the Fugitives and the Agrarians, Warren was a junior member in good standing. Among the New Critics, he assumed a central position. One of the distinguishing features of Warren's criticism, however, is that with its aesthetic formalism there is not combined that reactionary social ideology supported by many New Critics. New Critical methodology is reflected at a number of points in Warren's fictional practice, as might be demonstrated by comparing his definition of the philosophical novelist and the program for teaching poetry set down in *Understanding Poetry*. Thus, for example, the philosophical novelist is said not to be either schematic or deductive, while the proper treatment of poetry is defined as concrete and inductive. In his definition Warren emphasizes the union of "documentation of the world" and "generalization about values," while in *Understanding Poetry,* stress is laid on the poem as an organic system of relationships, the special poetic quality not inhering in any one factor taken in isolation.

On reflection, I wonder whether I have sufficiently illustrated my introductory claim: that Warren expertly combines the philosophical and the popular modes, each supporting the other. In my consideration of Warren as philosophical novelist, there is doubtless a danger, a danger to which all critics concerned with ideas are subject: that I have abstracted ideas from Warren's fiction and have thus reversed the artistic process, that is, the necessity to concretize, or indeed the need not just to put flesh on one's ideas, but to experience ideas only through and after the fleshly encounter. Warren writes only one kind of novel: there are no "entertainments" in the canon. He is an accomplished storyteller and a sophisticated critical intelligence. Even as one is caught up in the fast-paced action, violence, broad humor, sex and suspense of his novels, one responds to the philosophical novelist making "the same old struggle for his truth."

The Assumption of the "Burden" of History in *All the King's Men*

Murray Krieger

> I said, "But suppose there isn't anything to find?"
>   And the Boss said, "There is always something."
>   And I said, "Maybe not on the Judge."
>   And he said, "Man is conceived in sin and born in cor-
> ruption and he passeth from the stink of the didie to the
> stench of the shroud. There is always something."

It is a great leap in time and kind from Swift and Sterne to Robert
Penn Warren's *All the King's Men,* perhaps too great for the reader,
or for me, to manage. But I hope to show that this novel reveals the
human barnyard—the relation between the classic visionary and the
classic existent within the barnyard—in a way that I find in no other
work. For my purposes, this way, and thus this novel, are indispensable.

The barnyard concern that is at the center of *All the King's Men*
is at once evident from Willie Stark's judgment, quoted above. It is
a theodicy that he persuades our narrator, Jack Burden, to share with
him. Nor is it a difficult persuasion, since it is but a logical extension
of Burden's own philosophical and existential development. The
very first scene establishes the barnyard metaphor that dominates the
novel. Willie, now "the Boss," the all-dominating governor, is vis-
iting his old farm home. He comments on the pig trough he and Jack
are looking at:

From *The Classic Vision: The Retreat from Extremity in Modern Literature.* © 1971 by
the Johns Hopkins University Press.

"I bet I dumped ten thousand gallons of swill into that trough," he said, "one time and another." He let another glob of spit fall into the trough. "I bet I slopped five hundred head of hogs out of this trough," he said. "And," he said, "by God, I'm still doing it. Pouring swill."

"Well," I said, "swill is what they live on, isn't it?"

We see Jack adopt Willie's terminology and Willie's metaphor here, as well as his philosophy of man as a political animal: from here on both of them see the political life and the moral life as dominated by everyone's desire to control the pouring of the swill and to get into the trough himself, shoving aside any who stand in the way. Whatever can be done with man and for man must be done in recognition of the reality of this basic metaphor. So the language is recurrent in Jack's speech as well as in Willie's.

As we see from the tone of the opening quotation, Willie's barnyard doctrine derives from his Presbyterianism, which he tells us he has learned to make good use of to justify his ways to man. There are two major tenents which are not challenged—at least not until the very end of the novel. Man's nature is inherently and incorrigibly corrupt, indeed piggish; and man is predestined rather than free, so that he seeks only to fulfill his nature. This inevitability explains why you can dig up "dirt" about any man, even the Judge. It also explains why no one who wishes to "do business" can ignore our dirty, piggish nature; for, if he *is* to do business, he must do it by providing the opportunity for that nature to fulfill itself. Thus, like God, such a man makes use of our dirt, which one can hardly do by denying its existence as a part of us, as our essence.

Such predestined human depravity makes man ripe for positivistic manipulation, like the pig in search of the swill in his trough. And the man-god who can do the manipulating, in accordance with his special knowledge, at once wins the gift bestowed by his grateful fellows: absolute power and abject worship of that power. And their need for him is absolute. The process is much like that seen by the Grand Inquisitor projected by Ivan Karamazov: one must provide man not with freedom, but with miracle, mystery, and authority—combined with bread. Willie's commitment to action, his willingness to mess in the dirt (his own and that of others) which is the raw material of action, gives him control of the barnyard. He now can pour the swill to those who follow him, excluding "all those people who got pushed out of the trough." And he pours full and well. By allowing all the broad spectrum of men who come under his dominance to fulfill their natures in their various ways, he becomes irresistibly attractive to all: to corrupt men and to men of thought and even of puritanical moral conviction. Those ethical purists who distrust action because of the sour aftertaste of immoral necessities can act for Willie in a self-deceived purity of action, fulfilling their natures while he keeps hidden from them the dirty accompaniments which he is able to take on himself, for he knows the truth which their idealism cannot afford to confront. Of course, if what has been hidden should become apparent, then their purity will lead them to a shocked disavowal of political action once more. As Jack puts it, "Politics is action and all action is but a flaw in the perfection of inaction, which is peace." But Jack, our uncommitted, cynical narrator, can accept Willie's truth and the consequences of his worst action.

Jack's supposed father, the "Scholarly Attorney," is immune to all temptation of action, even Willie's sort that promises high results: "I will not touch the world of foulness again . . . that my hand shall come away with the stink on my fingers." These words remind us of Strephon's repulsion by foulness and Celia. Only a bit less insulated is Hugh Miller, who wants to lay about him with a baseball bat without defiling his hands with the accompanying moral filth, leaving it to Willie to keep it out of sight. So he must "welch" on the role he is committed to enact and must desert when his purity cannot put up with what Willie forces it to confront. The latter pattern is pretty much that of the clean surgeon, Adam Stanton, as well; he also will not face the moral (or rather immoral) consequences of what Willie's actions can accomplish in the incidental service of Adam's ethical objectives. All these hold-outs and hold-backs refuse to partake of this grand barnyard scheme, which is both the political extension of a total pragmatic positivism and the perverse projection of Calvinist fundamentalism. Such is not the case with Jack, who—in his cynicism—neither holds out from Willie nor holds back from the moral consequences once he joins him.

Insofar as Willie's Calvinist doctrine—so convenient to his program of action—rests upon a conception of man as an easily fed stimulus-response mechanism, it accords fully with the philosophical movement of Jack Burden, historian, from "Idealism" to the "Great Sleep" to the "Great Twitch." The reduction from the moral to the crudely factual, together with the acceptance of the latter in its most unelevated reality, is as much an assumption of Jack's positivism as it is of Willie's authoritarian benevolence, cynically based, as it is, on his perversion of Calvinist theology. This dedication to the crudest of our subhuman facts does not contradict Jack's early affiliation with the doctrine he terms his idealism ("life as motion"), despite the fact that this idealism persuades him not only of the unreality of all that is beyond the reach of his vision but even of the essential unreality of what he sees, inasmuch as it all depends upon his consciousness. From here it is a small step for him to doubt that he himself is real, except as a bundle of sensory receptacles. No wonder that he is ready to see all human values reduced to empirical fact—indeed, in the end, to neurological fact (whatever the ontological status of these "facts").

Jack's idealism makes him ready for the Great Sleep which deadens so much of his life. He fails Anne early, disappointing her young hopes by his lack of commitment to any future, or even any serious interest in it. True to the Scholarly Attorney he supposes to be his father, he has an aimlessness in his youth that is already a kind of sleep. As we recall the recurrent image of purity represented in his mind by the young Anne in the water on the day of that idyllic picture, we see Anne playing the unavailable mermaid to Jack's Prufrock, a young but already played-out Prufrock of the twilight world of the Old Dominion. Having sleepily failed Anne, he fails the dead Cass Mastern with a more complete indulgence in the Great Sleep. He can momentarily emerge long enough to substitute—like a careless Meursault—Lois's sensualism for his more mysterious "sea-girl." This act (his marriage to Lois) is an extension and a proof of his idealism, with its reduction of reality (only half believed in) to what the senses receive. Only momentarily revived, he lapses into sleep again. Jack is ready for Willie, whose activism makes him insistently real. Willie answers Jack's need, as he answers the needs of all those about him whom he implicates in his willful destiny—a destiny that is, as we shall see, founded on the reduction of others to a will-less response itself produced by the power of his will. Willie thus comes to be the medium of Jack's expression, the shaper of his language, and—as activist—the logical realization of Jack's negativism, his cynical sense of reality.

When his service to this reality, under Willie's godlike tutelage, results in Anne's becoming Willie's mistress, Jack is ready for the ultimate realization that human value is reducible to involuntary neurological response: the Great Sleep has become the Great Twitch. He now feels that it was foolish for him to substitute Lois for Anne, since Lois and Anne were really the same after all. All distinctions among patterns and values of human behavior are now collapsed into the identity of the Twitch. How, then, could he have been so scrupulous about Anne and what he thought was her love for her "Jackie-Bird"?

> She hadn't loved him, but had merely had a mysterious itch in the blood and he was handy and the word *love* was a word for the mysterious itch. [Her] withholdments and hesitations were no better or worse than the hottest surrender nor better or worse than those withholdments practiced by Lois for other ends. And in the end you could not tell Anne Stanton from Lois Seager, for they were alike, and though the mad poet William Blake wrote a poem to tell the Adversary who is Prince of This World that He could not ever change Kate into Nan, the mad poet was quite wrong, for anybody could change Kate into Nan, or if indeed the Prince couldn't change Kate into Nan it was only because Kate and Nan were exactly alike to begin with and were, in fact, the same with only the illusory difference of name, which meant nothing, for names meant nothing and all the words we speak meant nothing and there was only the pulse in the blood and the twitch of the nerve, like a dead frog's leg in the experiment when the electric current goes through.

So "The Great Twitch" becomes Jack's ultimate vision, the end of the historian's history: "So I fled west from the fact, and in the West, at the end of History, the Last Man on that Last Coast, on my hotel bed, I had discovered the dream. That dream was the dream that all life is but the dark heave of blood and the twitch of the nerve."

Here, at the end of his flight from history, Jack finds freedom from his responsibility, from guilt. "The words *Anne Stanton* were simply a name for a peculiarly complicated piece of mechanism which should mean nothing whatsoever to Jack Burden, who himself was simply another rather complicated piece of mechanism." Under the sublime indifference of fact, Jack discovers an innocence not very different from Meursault's: "nothing was your fault or anybody's fault, for things are always as they are." Unlike Ivan Karamazov sitting in judgment of himself, Jack can assert that "you are never guilty of a crime which you did not commit. So there is innocence and a new start in the West, after all." On his ride back East Jack's confidence in his neurological reduction is confirmed for him by the twitch in the cheek of his elderly companion, the independent twitch with a life of its own, livelier than the face which bears it. So, Jack concludes, the twitch is all; and, more mysteriously, the twitch itself comes to know that it is all there really is. In this way, Jack, who like everything else is "all twitch," can come to "the secret knowledge" that this is so. Thus "the twitch can know that the twitch is all."

The utter reduction of man, of himself, is complete, the lower-than-barnyard gift that confers freedom. Jack is ripe to become the involved—almost obsessed—witness to the prefrontal lobectomy shortly to be performed by Adam Stanton. What better confirmation of man's twitching essence than the fact that brain-burning can transform personality and even remove moral awareness? Jack forces himself to witness the operation, allows himself a last disturbance over the fact "that the burning brain had a smell like the burning horses." When it is over, with enough of the brain burned away, "the little pieces of brain which had been cut out were put away to think their little thoughts quietly somewhere among the garbage, and what was left inside the split-open skull of the gaunt individual was sealed back up and left to think up an entirely new personality." And Jack suggests a baptism: "for he is born again and not of woman. I baptize thee in the name of the Big Twitch, the Little Twitch, and the Holy Ghost. Who, no doubt, is a Twitch, too."

Cass Mastern, Jack's elusive historical subject, possessed of a profound moral conscience, long before found himself on the path toward something like Jack's notion of the Twitch. As he observes the ease with which he is drawn to an adulterous relationship with Annabelle Trice, wife of his friend, Cass questions the basis of his previous morality: "Therefore what virtue and honor I had known in the past had been an accident of habit and not the fruit of the will." But, unlike Jack, Cass cannot accept this dreadful freedom from guilt. It is, rather, his nature to move on, through extremity, to re-earn his belief in the moral capacity of man. For him there can be no resting in the Great Twitch of neurological habit. This is what prevents Jack from understanding Cass well enough to complete his work on him. Jack gives up the task and enters the Great Sleep "because he was afraid to understand for what might be understood there was a reproach to him." It is a failure of his moral imagination. In contrast to Cass, who "learned that the world is all of one piece," Jack saw the world only as "an accumulation of items, odds and ends of things like the broken and misused and dust-shrouded things gathered in a garret. Or it was a flux of things before his eyes (or behind his eyes) and one thing had nothing to do, in the end, with anything else."

The story of Cass Mastern, then, makes demands upon Jack beyond what his historian's role has expected or can handle. And he fails in this first of his researches. Facts are not enough to reach to the moral imagination of a Cass Mastern; and Jack—both idealist and positivist—is restricted to morally insignificant, uninterrelated facts. Jack's painful development in the novel—and his earlier resistance to that development—are alike centered in his relation both to history and to *his* history (and Cass, as at once forebear *and* historical subject, represents both to him). How is Jack to relate himself to the past and to *his* past when he cannot find a moral relationship among facts and cannot move beyond facts? Nor can he move beyond the determinism of fact to the free act of will. So, inheritor of the world of Cass Mastern and (as he wrongly believes) of the Scholarly Attorney, he is Burden-ed by a history he cannot undo, even if he will not undertake the moral responsibility of accepting it.

Jack's second research is of another sort, concerned as it is with fact alone. How, then, can he—with the commitments we know him to have—be other than successful? Indeed, he is a smashing success: little is left standing in the wake of that success. Having come out of his Great Sleep to join Willie and having committed himself (though in his essentially uncommitted way) to Willie, Jack the factual historian is given his assignment. He is to dig up some dirt on Judge Irwin, his boyhood idol and (almost) foster-father. And when he questions whether there is anything to dig up on the Judge, Willie answers with the adaptation of Presbyterianism ("from the stink of the didie to the stench of the shroud") which furnished the opening quotation for this chapter. Thus Jack enters upon his second job of historical research, the "Case of the Upright Judge." This one is tailored to Willie's coldly political objectives, as it is cut to the dimensions of Willie's theology; thus it is limited by the factual requirements of Jack's idealism-positivism. So Jack becomes the paragon of objective "historical researchers" ("we love truth") as he proceeds to teach Anne and Adam—and himself a history lesson.

His historian's love for "truth," for the unmitigated fact that invariably turns out ugly, is a match for Willie's. We must remember that Willie never asked him to frame the Judge with untruths or half-truths: Willie only asked him to dig up the dirty truth that was surely there, hidden (and discoverable) somewhere. "You don't ever have to frame anybody, because the truth is always sufficient," Willie tells Jack. Having dug up a truth that turns out to dirty the memory of former Governor Stanton as well as his friend, the upright Judge, Jack puts it to work on Adam as well as on Anne: "I had found the truth, I had dug the truth up out of the ash pile, the garbage heap, the kitchen midden, the bone yard, and had sent that little piece of truth to Adam Stanton. I couldn't cut the truth to match his ideas. Well, he'd have to make his ideas match the truth. That is what all of us historical researchers believe. The truth shall make you free."

Though Adam and Anne do not go quite as far as that Meursault-like conclusion, they both do cave in, Adam by foregoing his scruples to go to work for Willie and Anne by becoming Willie's mistress. The truth has worked to put everything in the order required to bring about the catastrophe of Willie's assassination (with, of course, Adam's subsequent death). And the catastrophe, in turn, accumulates in Jack a burden of guilt that even he can no longer evade. For whatever the sneaky Duffy may have done to put the gun in Adam's hand, Jack must come to know how thoroughly the responsibility for it is his own, as the value-free, positivistic "historical researcher." He will come to see what there had been in the Cass Mastern research to reproach him as he learns what there was in the Judge Irwin research that had to destroy morally the very success which its presuppositions guaranteed. Like Cass but unlike himself under the rule of the Great Twitch, Jack learns that one *can* be guilty of a crime which he did not commit.

We can see, then, that the dehumanized history of Judge Irwin, as Jack discovers it—in almost detective-story fashion—becomes the primary action for the fictional structure that is this novel (presumably written as fact by Jack). It is worth noting in some detail the ways in which Warren (or rather Jack, his fictive narrator) transforms factual history into human history, that is, transforms biography into novel, the chronological chain of events into Aristotelian fable. The primary justification for what is included and the order of its inclusion is its place in the action rather than its role in the unfolding of Willie Stark's life and career. Indeed, we can ask to what extent this is Willie's story and to what extent Jack permits himself to move from his merely visionary role to usurp the place of protagonist.

It is perhaps appropriate, as we treat such matters, to note that the real Huey Long has been often seen as the historical basis for Willie Stark, so that Warren has been seen as writing a political pseudo-novel about the real Louisiana from his outpost at the state university. Those who read the work carefully should be persuaded by it to accept the author's disclaimers of such an intention, even as we recognize the biographical and political realities in the "germ" of the novel. But Warren has overcome the biographical and political realities of the Huey Long epoch and its cataclysmic end; he has overcome them as Jack Burden, in his story, overcomes the biographical and political pseudo-realities of the Willie Stark epoch and its cataclysmic end. If this were only Governor Stark's story, a make-believe biography, then Willie could be a stand-in for Governor Long. But, as an Aristotelian action, it is the story of neither.

At the very opening we must note the care with which Warren (or must we not say Jack?) begins at the beginning of the action rather than at the beginning of the career. We are not to confuse the beginning, middle, and end of Willie's story with the beginning, middle, and end of the story which is the structural whole that concerns us. The novel starts on the day that culminates in the unsatisfactory visit to Judge Irwin and Willie's consequent order to Jack to start digging for the inevitable dirt. All the major developments in the plot have their beginnings here. It is only after he, in chapter 1, has launched the action on that day in 1936 (*in medias res*) that our narrator can turn back, in chapter 2, to the chronological beginnings of Willie's story in 1922. First things first; and our narrator makes clear what comes first with him, just as he must carry his story to an end well beyond the end of Willie's story. Further, before he feels free to fill us in on the background, the biographical beginnings, he must also make it clear (in the final words of chapter 1 and the first words of chapter 2) that he is writing in 1939—three years after that day—and that most of the characters who figured in the opening of the tale (Masters, Adam Stanton, Judge Irwin, and Willie himself) are dead. So the tale is in a specially definitive sense finished by this time, before we enter upon its chronological beginning, whose subordinate place has now been assured. And there is a suggestion of catastrophe in its being finished, a catastrophe that, as is intimated by the final words of chapter 1 ("Little Jackie made it stick, all right"), grows out of the plot elements unleashed in that first chapter.

Almost everything does grow out of Jack's research on the "upright judge," which Willie, at the end of the first chapter, charges him to undertake so that Willie may have the potential blackmail to influence the Judge's future political behavior. His research produces the facts about Judge Irwin's acceptance of a bribe and about Governor Stanton's complicity in protecting his guilty friend and political sidekick. Jack first uses these facts to persuade Adam to take Willie's hospital position. Without meaning to, he has also helped persuade Anne to become Willie's mistress. When, at a propitious moment, Duffy sees to it that Adam learns what his sister has become, Adam assassinates Willie and is killed himself. In the meantime Jack has also tried to use the facts in order to blackmail the Judge, but Irwin kills himself. Yet strangely, ironically, the success of Jack's research, with all these dreadful consequences, can lead to *his* salvation. The "bright, beautiful, silvery soprano scream" of Jack's mother when she learns of the suicide turns the book around by giving Jack a new fact—the actual identity of Irwin as his father—and a new sense of the sort of humanity she has been capable of during the many years of his contempt for her.

So the fable has an Aristotelian completeness to it, although it must be seen as casting Jack, rather than Willie, in the role of protagonist. Indeed, so far are we from mere history or biography that we can note the traditional form which the fable has been given: the search for identity takes on the literalness of the search for one's parentage. Like many of literature's oldest heroes, Jack must discover who his father really is—a man crucially different from his apparent father—and who his mother really is (although this is a discovery of internal rather than external facts about her identity). And this discovery is central to his discovery of who *he* can really be. So much of what Jack has been seems to be a reflection of the Scholarly Attorney, his supposed father, and his superficially flighty mother that his sense of his own identity must be profoundly changed by the twin discoveries which the "silvery soprano scream" forces him to make. It is this internal development, this self-discovery, that enables Jack, instead of one of the more fixed characters who surround him, to become the protagonist of the tale.

But Jack is narrator as well as protagonist. In tracing the origin and development of the novel, Warren tells us that it began as a play and that, with its transformation into a novel, there arose the "necessity for a character of a higher degree of self-consciousness than my politician, a character to serve as a kind of commentator and *raisonneur* and chorus." He also acknowledges what I have pointed out, that "the story, in a sense, became the story of Jack Burden, the teller of the tale." Warren's "desire to avoid writing a straight naturalistic novel, the kind of novel that the material so readily invited"—his desire, in other words, to be more than historian—led to his need for the perspective that the mock-historian, Burden, could give him as he proceeded to free himself from the historian's factual confines. As Jack frees himself from factual historicity, so the novel frees itself of its biographical encumbrance. But Jack's freeing of himself is a story in itself—*the* story—which has him as its protagonist.

If, in his desire to transform the play into a work that was truly novelistic, Warren invented a narrator who was at least a semi-protagonist even as he was "commentator and *raisonneur* and chorus," he had, in that invention, venerable literary precedent. Jack Burden is, in effect, playing Marlow to Willie Stark's Mr. Kurtz. Nor is it inappropriate for us to look for Conradian parallels in Warren, who in more than one way seems technically indebted to the novelist about whom he has written so sensitively. I have noted, in Warren's disposition of his first two chapters, the extent to which he permits Jack to manipulate—at times to jumble—the time sequence of events in order to make it his tale rather than history's. The darting back and leaping ahead in time, seemingly at will but actually for good fictional purposes, continue throughout Jack's recital, and in ways similar to Marlow's manipulation of the chronology of events in *Lord Jim*. In both works, mere events are worked about in order to make certain that human form and meaning predominate over the accidental, "straight naturalistic" facts in their accidental, "straight naturalistic" order. Both novels are also quite ready to reveal in advance how the affair turns out—Jack tells us in his first chapter who is to be dead by the time of his writing three short years later—so that the factual suspense that asks "What happened?" can be subordinated to the more profound, and less easily settled, human issues that they wish to concentrate upon. Such arranging indicates how far Jack-as-narrator, like Marlow, has moved from the bald historicity of his second research (into Judge Irwin), from his subservience to the bald inhumanity of raw fact. For we must not forget that it is the latest Jack, the Jack who emerges at the end of the book, who has written the book we have by then concluded.

If by the conclusion Jack, as protagonist, has changed from the earlier Jack, it must be that he has moved beyond the Great Twitch, despite everything in his positivism and in his devotion to the positivistic sort of history he can understand that seems to point to that final secret knowledge he called the Great Twitch. For him it is not to be final after all. Yet it is not what he seems at first to have done to Anne and to Adam by revealing the freedom-giving truths of factual history that turns him from the Twitch. Quite the contrary: it is during his flight to California, after Anne admits she has become Willie's mistress, that he first discovers the final liberating truth bestowed by the Twitch. Anne's confession allows him—by absolving himself of complicity—to equate her with Lois. Even the suicide of Irwin might not have turned him from liberation to a sense of his own guilt—though he might have recognized the parallel between his responsibility for Irwin's suicide and Irwin's responsibility for Mortimer Littlepaugh's suicide (which helps cause Irwin's own) or Cass Mastern's responsibility for Duncan Trice's (which precipitates Cass's own abandonment to extremity). But, as I have already noted, Jack begins to be turned around at the moment of Aristotelian discovery and peripety, the "bright, beautiful, silvery soprano scream" followed by the revelation of his parentage by his mother. Further, to his responsibility for Irwin's suicide one must soon add his responsibility—only slightly more indirect—for the killings of Willie and Adam. These responsibilities, now far more extensive than those of Cass or Irwin, might well carry him beyond the capacity of the Great Twitch to keep him innocent, might well defy its principle that "you are never guilty of a crime which you did not commit."

Jack finally refuses to act upon this principle when he turns away from his chance to take revenge upon Duffy as the arranger of Willie's death. As he learns the truth from Sadie Burke and threatens the new Governor Duffy with his knowledge, he admits to us, "I felt like a million because I thought it let me out. Duffy was the villain and I was the avenging hero." But each time he feels like "St. George and the dragon" or "Jesus Christ with the horsewhip in the temple," he feels sick from an acid taste in the back of his mouth. For he recognizes his fellowship with Duffy: "It was as though in the midst of the scene Tiny Duffy had slowly and like a brother winked at me with his oyster eye and I had known he knew the nightmare truth, which was that we were twins bound together. . . . We were bound together forever and I could never hate him without hating myself or love myself without loving him. We were bound together under the unwinking eye of Eternity and by the Holy Grace of the Great Twitch whom we must all adore." Only one more step is required. Sugar-Boy's appearance gives Jack the chance to have Duffy killed as Duffy had Willie killed: by the merest whisper of a name to a desperate man with a loaded gun. But the thought of the resemblance between the act he contemplates and Duffy's act makes Jack's awareness of their fellowship complete. About to name him to Sugar-Boy as Willie's killer, again he envisions the wink of that fellowship passing between them: "I saw Duffy's face, large and lunar and sebaceous, nodding at me as at the covert and brotherly appreciation of a joke, and even as I opened my lips to speak the syllables of his name, he winked. He winked right at me like a brother." It is much like Ivan Karamazov's discovery of his feelings about Smerdyakov, from whose basest act he cannot separate himself. Jack can deny the Great Twitch, the power that denies all distinctions, only by insisting upon distinguishing himself from Duffy. So at the last moment he draws back: at an enormous risk to his own life—now exposed to Sugar-Boy's fury as he knows it will be—Jack names no one and treats the entire affair as a joke. But Sugar-Boy, almost miraculously, spares Jack: " 'I-I-I durn near d-d-done it.' I ran my tongue over my dry lips. 'I know it,' I said." Jack has run a moral risk because he would rather die for Duffy than remain his brother.

So Jack is not Duffy, and he has proved it. Not only has he refused to authorize Duffy's murder, but he has refused in the one way most dangerous to his own safey. Like the captain at the end of Conrad's *Secret Sharer* who steers his ship closer to the shore than good seamanship would permit—and closer than his "double," Leggatt, requires—Jack's reckless withdrawal is in part a gratuitous gesture that bears courageous testimony to moral strength. None of what he has done before is changed by this act; indeed, he is now capable of feeling his guilt in all that has transpired. But, free of the Great Twitch, free to face the responsibility of his part in the universal complicity, he is obliged to make distinctions once again, distinctions between himself and Duffy, between Anne and Lois, between Adam and Willie. With respect to man's capacity for evil, the all-or-none alternative of a puritanism turned sour has now given way to an infinite variety of possible degrees of goodness or badness.

Jack need not deny the barnyard claims about man—Willie's, like Gulliver's—for him, like Swift, to acknowledge that in the herd we may find some surprising and gratifying actions. And these must be noted too. It is, after all, what Cass Mastern had discovered before him. No wonder that Jack shortly declares himself ready to return to the story of Cass.

We have seen that the extravagance of Jack's gesture in preventing Duffy from being killed is just such a surprising and gratifying action. Clearly Jack is getting ready to return to the herd, while preserving his distinction-making power, as he helps the herd to write its history. But now, of course, his will be a different sort of history, with a different hierarchy of values. Even factual truth may have to go. Because Jack has been an historian so faithful to fact, his lies will be believed. We have seen Sugar-Boy accept his lie that he had no further information about Willie's killer. In addition, the final words we see him speak to his mother represent a major untruth, although it helps to preserve the sort of being she has come to be for Jack since the moment of her "silvery soprano scream." It is a lie about Judge Irwin's last moments, a lie reminiscent of the earth-shaking one Marlow speaks to Kurtz's "intended" at the end of *Heart of Darkness*. While Kurtz's final words were "The horror! The horror!" Marlow tells the bereaved woman that his final words were her name; while Irwin's suicide stems from the newly resurrected facts about the evils of his political past, Jack tells his mother it was caused by nothing more damning than the depression related to failing health. He expressly denies any lingering history of wrongdoing on Irwin's part and, when there is some suggestion of doubts in her, he can even—little-boy style—"swear to God" that he speaks the truth. Marlow's profound abhorrence of lies gave his lie a special significance; Jack's ruthless fidelity to the cruelty of fact here guarantees that he will be believed. It also makes clear his new attitude to the truth, and makes clear the rejection of the Twitch, a rejection which this new attitude requires.

The truth of the Great Twitch, then, might set one morally free by equating all men as brothers in their automatic neurological responses. But it is not this truth which can allow one to rest with others' eyes upon him in mute condemnation, even the condemnation that proceeds out of brotherhood. Only the return to distinctions in degree, to crucial differences of more or less among human actions, can allow one to accept the consequences of behavior, including the consequence of being looked at by one's fellows. It may lead to an awareness of guilt, but one can accept the possibility of being more or less guilty once he admits that, even if everyone is doomed to be guilty, everyone is also free—under "the agony of will"—to be guilty in different ways. We have seen that Jack's need to deprive Duffy of the right to bestow upon him the wink of brotherhood led him to play a dangerous game with Sugar-Boy rather than to play Duffy's game against Duffy.

Earlier, we remember, it was just such a wink of fellowship that initially sealed the bone between Willie and Jack as they launched the political career founded on notions of the barnyard and on the Twitch that, theoretically, accounted for the equal and constant lowly state of the barnyard members. From Willie to Duffy: the wink binds Jack to those serving, with him, "the Holy Grace of the Great Twitch whom we must all adore." But the wink he welcomed from Willie he must reject from Duffy. Now he will be able to bear Duffy's eyes upon him and not feel them winking, now that he has acted to deny the truth of the Twitch. He will be able to assert, not only his own moral superiority to Duffy, but Willie's. This permits Jack the belief which he must maintain: that Willie was a great man, whatever else he may also have been. Similarly, we have seen, he can maintain that Judge Irwin was a just judge and a strong man—an admirable man—whatever evil he may have committed. The abandonment of all-or-none, the acceptance of human imperfection and the variety of degrees with which it expresses itself or is modified, encourages the beginning of a moral life that permits men to look upon one another without fearing the knowing smirk that disguises itself as a wink. Yet the relaxed acceptance of the looks of men—so far from the realm of austere judgment that looks *at* men—is well beyond the ethical and into the classic.

Other characters are also troubled by eyes turned upon them. The long trail of Cass Mastern's tragedy is largely impelled by the fact that his partner in adultery, Annabelle Trice, cannot tolerate the accusation in the eyes of her slave, Phebe, and, in desperation, sells her. Cass, who like Jack must prove that virtue is possible and is not merely a euphemism for habit, requires himself to follow her path in order to buy and free her. When he fails, he sets his own slaves free, though he is troubled by the further sorrows into which he feels he is sending them. Though he can take no moral credit for what he has done, still it is better than living with his sense of their eyes upon him:

> They had kissed my hands and wept for joy, but I could take no part in their rejoicing. I had not flattered myself that I had done anything for them. What I had done I had done for myself, to relieve my spirit of a burden, the burden of their misery and their eyes upon me. The wife of my dead friend had found the eyes of the girl Phebe upon her and had gone wild and had ceased to be herself and had sold the girl into misery. I had found their eyes upon me and had freed them into misery, lest I should do worse. For many cannot bear their eyes upon them, and enter into evil and cruel ways in their desperation.

Gilbert Mastern, successful and worldly brother of Cass, scorns the young man's impracticality as absurd and is offended at the thought of a fallow plantation, one which Cass will not sell, though he has no one to work it. Gilbert's reaction is a classic one: "My God, man, it is land, don't you understand, it is land, and land cries out for man's hand." Cass himself sees Gilbert as having a specially endowed worldliness which even permitted him to be a beneficent slaveowner: "Perhaps only a man like my brother Gilbert can in the midst of evil retain enough of innocence and strength to bear their eyes upon him and to do a little justice in the terms of the great injustice."

If he sounds a bit like Judge Irwin, it is probably because he is meant to. In the final paragraphs of the novel, Jack describes himself turning once more to the life of Cass Mastern in hopes of having been granted a new understanding that will allow him to re-create himself as a historian. And he comments upon the strange juxtaposition of Cass Mastern and Judge Irwin: "I suppose that there is some humor in the fact that while I write about Cass Mastern I live in the house of Judge Irwin and eat bread bought with his money. For Judge Irwin and Cass Mastern do not resemble each other very closely. (If Judge Irwin resembles any Mastern it is Gilbert, the granite-headed brother of Cass)." It is rather the Scholarly Attorney, Ellis Burden, who resembles Cass, while Jack, who thought himself the inheritor of the weakness of his supposed father, has acted in ways analogous to Cass. But now Jack emerges morally in a way that is even more positive and surely less tragic than Cass's. Indeed it is altogether untragic. But the juxtaposition of Cass and Irwin which Jack notes here at the end, as he writes the story of Cass in the house of Irwin, marks the joining of the two widely differing subjects of Jack's previous historical researchs. And the Jack who now emerges into the world, like the book now being completed under his pen, unites them by extending their history into the metahistorical human world of freedom.

As we see from Jack's unconscious search for his parentage, his history is bound up with his surname. Although Warren never explicitly plays with Jack's name, I should like to for a moment, for it plays a symbolic role in his position at the end. What has happened is that he comes to accept that name and its meaning at the point where he no longer has to. Much of what he has gone through in his earlier "stages along life's way" he has gone through as a result of his being a Burden: he thinks himself Ellis Burden's son, and Cass Mastern, as well as being his historical subject, is an uncle of that supposed father. But now that Jack has discovered that Ellis Burden is not his father, now that he can be free of the historical burden of being a Burden, he assumes that burden (Burden). He even brings Ellis Burden to live with him, as he never could have done before. In his own words, but without explicit reference to his name (though surely the pun is there), he justifies his present attitude to Anne: "I tried to tell her how if you could not accept the past and its burden there was no future, for without one there cannot be the other, and how if you could accept the past you might hope for the future, for only out of the past can you make the future."

Jack has come to terms with history—and with *his* history— freeing himself from it in order, as a free man, to accept it. "History is blind, but man is not," he approvingly quotes Hugh Miller as saying. However, doomed man must live "in the agony of will," for the irreversibility of past facts does not make the future irreversible until it has happened. Man is not free of guilt, as under the Great Twitch, but he *is* free to be guilty (and not *only* guilty) and free to learn to live with *that* freedom. This double sense of being free of history only by being bound to it is what permits the final words of the novel, which describe the future of Jack and Anne: "soon now we shall go out of the house and go into the convulsion of the world, out of history into history and the awful responsibility of Time." With Anne, who by marrying him has also assumed the surname that she need not have assumed, he takes on Burden just as he is free to allow it to fall from him.

Jack Burden is for me a unique narrator (and *All the King's Men* a uniquely useful novel) because the existential development he undergoes permits me to see him as running the gamut of my categories. He first goes through what I have seen as the general pattern of apparently similar narrators. Like Marlow with his Kurtz or his Jim, or Ishmael with his Ahab, or Zeitblom with his Leverkühn, Jack appears to be the fictive narrator who creates and aesthetically sustains for us the self-destructive career of the tragic existent, here Willie Stark. Of course, Jack is less morally dedicated a narrator than the others: he is not a representative of ethical existence as is a Marlow or a Leverkühn. Still, like his counterparts, Jack is to be a tragic visionary rather than a tragic existent himself. Although the fictive narrator must assimilate his creature aesthetically, he does not dare replace him existentially. The narrator may threaten to become the protagonist himself, as in *Heart of Darkness;* but it is precisely as the tragic visionary who pulls back from the unmitigated indulgence in tragic existence that he does so. It is in this sense that we saw Jack choose Willie out of his need, his lack, so that Willie can be his existential agent, acting out his cynical principles. But when, on that bed in Long Beach, California, Jack commits himself to the utter nihilism of the Great Twitch, no longer flinching from its deadening consequences, he is ready to move—almost with less reservation than even Willie—to the state of being a tragic existent himself.

When Jack draws back from the ultimate act of having Duffy killed precisely in the way Duffy had Willie killed—merely by allowing himself to speak a word, a reflex action that would produce another, deadly reflex action—and when he discovers the reason for his drawing back, he is, in effect, rejecting the Great Twitch. He finally can see the Great Twitch as only a reduction, a metaphor for our barnyard behavior, but a metaphor which our humanity must struggle to elude if it is to assert, however sporadically, its freedom. And he must measure our humanity by its capacity to engage its messy, unpredictable reality, a reality that overruns our neat, metaphorical boundaries and thus demonstrates the insufficiency of the metaphor, although not quite to the point of denying its cogency.

So Jack has moved beyond the tragic, now as a classic visionary. He understands anew the role of history and man's responsibility to himself and to it: he understands the subtle dimensions of the historical community and its demands, as forces springing from solid reality. At last he may be able to make sense of a scene he once witnessed (early in the novel) which moved him deeply enough for him to recall it, poignantly, much later. From the window of a train moving through empty country, in which some insubstantial houses seem very temporarily to have been dropped, Jack sees the figure of a faceless woman come to the back door of a house, fling some water from a pan she is carrying, and go back into the house. Jack feels that she has gone back where "she is going to stay," back to "the secret" that is inside. This is her place: it is not she or her house that is temporary but Jack, who is running away with no place to "stay." "And all at once you feel like crying. But the train is going fast, and almost immediately whatever you felt is taken away from you, too." Even the feeling of aimless desperation cannot stay. Jack, the Idealist, with his exclusive claim about "life as motion," is thus confronted by this solid chunk of immovable reality. Later, at an important moment, he recalls the woman who "deliberately" entered the house, who was "not going to run away," who was "going into the house to some secret which is there, some knowledge." When he first witnessed the scene from the moving train, he did not comprehend its appeal to him; and when he thought about it during the later train ride returning him from California and his discovery of the Great Twitch, he rejected its significance, since he claimed a "secret knowledge" all his own (of the dominance of the Great Twitch) that superseded the woman's "secret knowledge." But if, after the final Duffy episode, he can come closer to this other secret knowledge—to the woman's sense of place, of solid reality—he still does so only from the outside, as a visionary, though he is clearly in the realm of the classic. It is the woman—or her counterpart in the story, Lucy Stark—who is the classic existent.

But when Jack returns at the end and permits himself to live in Judge Irwin's house, when he takes Ellis Burden to live with him in that house, when he marries Anne, when he prepares to enter politics once more to work for a similarly rejuvenated Hugh Miller, when he declares himself ready to return to the Cass Mastern materials in order at last to master them, when Anne and he, having lived in the Irwin house, now feel themselves free also to decide to leave it ("out of history into history")—all these decisions find him entering classic existence itself. I know of no other work in which so sophisticated, so self-conscious a life-scarred creature—especially a narrator-creator of a monumentally tragic figure—wills himself into such a simplicity of final commitments and comes close to getting away with it. Jack the narrator records, with a considerable sense of identity, Jack and his Anne walking off—but hardly idyllically, in view of all they know and accept about themselves and the world—into the future, into the history to come (which is partially free) out of the darkly bound history behind them. Certainly they do enter as existents themselves, as agents. It is a daring stroke, this walking off into the sunset (sunrise?); but, in view of what we know of Jack Burden, what we know he knows, it is—I believe—more daring than sentimental.

After all, it is this Jack who is presumably finishing the book we have been reading in the little time remaining before he is to leave the Irwin house with Anne. The writing of his book, like the writing of his Cass Mastern study, is his farewell to his status as classic visionary and the preparation for his departure as classic existent. This book, a mock-biography that turns confessional and autobiographical, has been written by the most recent Jack Burden, the Jack Burden of its last pages. So the events of the book have been the education that permitted his writing the book. This education has permitted him to triumph over the facticity of history. It has permitted him to find human vindication even in the disastrous results of his heartless research on Judge Irwin, which is the basic action of his fable. This action thus becomes the enabling act for him to write the Cass Mastern story, as the Cass Mastern story will be the enabling act for him to leave the historian's visionary role for the actor's existential role. In this way the technical point of view upon action merges with action, aesthetics merges with thematics, history merges with a free present: in short, vision merges with existence. So far can the modest classic vision try to reach toward union when the barnyard is most richly conscious of itself.

The American Novelist
and American History:
A Revaluation of *All the King's Men*

Richard Gray

Robert Penn Warren is a writer of extraordinarily diverse talents and interests. He is, among other things, one of the founders of the New Criticism, a poet and a poetic dramatist of national reputation (he won both the Pulitzer Prize and the National Book Award for his nineteen volumes of verse), and a gifted teacher. Above all, though, he is a writer whose moral and philosophical bias is towards the kind of historical specificity and social density which is perhaps the special preserve of the novel. This more than anything else accounts for the exceptional range and volume of his fictional writing and for the usual association of his name with one book in particular which is, by common consent, his finest achievement: *All the King's Men,* first published in 1946. Occasionally, a case has been made for the superiority of one of his other novels, and there have been one or two attempts to locate the centre of his work in the poetry. But these have been scattered, infrequent, and in the event, I think unconvincing. *All the King's Men* remains his masterwork, and perhaps his most characteristic piece of fiction too, so that any assessment of Warren the imaginative writer has ultimately to focus upon it.

As soon as anyone begins to discuss *All the King's Men,* of course, he is immediately confronted with a difficulty which is becoming commonplace in the field of American literature. The difficulty is one of saying something fresh about a book which has already been so exhaustively, and even exhaustingly, covered. On the one

From *Journal of American Studies* 6, no. 3 (December 1972). © 1972 by Cambridge University Press.

hand, there have been so many analyses of image and symbol in *All the King's Men,* and its handling of narrative point-of-view, that the reader may begin to suspect Warren of what F. R. Leavis, in another context, once called an excessive amount of "doing." On the other, there have been almost as many commentaries which have as their purpose a rebuttal of Warren's apparent reading of history, and more specifically the history of the Louisiana demagogue Huey Long on whom the character of Willie Stark was based. Behind these lies the assumption that Warren has taken the given facts and distorted them almost, but not quite, beyond recognition.

These, I think, have been the two major tendencies in criticism of *All the King's Men* since its first publication, and perhaps the simple mentioning of them suggests the vacuum which still exists and possibilities of approach which remain to be pursued. There have been many, perhaps too many, analyses of the novel which set it in some vast ahistorical context in order to pay compliment to Warren's handling of the techniques of fiction. In such cases, the critic assumes that the book is written in a kind of code which it is his task to crack. When he does crack it, or some part of it, he seems so pleased with his success that the value or validity of the message thus communicated hardly engages his interest. To be more exact, the uses to which history and specific social circumstances are put in *All the King's Men,* and the larger meanings Warren extracts from all this, are rarely brought into question. The writer is accepted on the basis of his more obviously symbolic intentions, without reference to some of the rather dubious means by which those intentions are fulfilled, and the result is frequently commentary like the following:

> The symbolic fable of this book embodies the world of fact in Willie Stark ("stark" fact) and the world of idea or abstraction in Adam (innocence of the world of fact) Stanton, while the Eves of the piece, Anne Stanton and Sadie Burke, are the agents by which knowledge of evil is transmitted to Jack Burden (who must finally bear the full burden of knowledge, as he is regenerated).
>
> (John M. Bradbury, *The Fugitives*)

The point about such commentary is that it isolates *All the King's Men* from those powers of history which supply the spine of its narrative and the centre of its interests and, in doing so, it inevitably distorts and impoverishes the meaning of the book. Supposing what is said here to be true, the reader would surely be justified in asking why so much praise has been showered upon Warren; and, more particularly, for what reason Warren should have felt himself impelled to adopt a set of given historical circumstances only to alter them.

This is precisely what other commentators on *All the King's Men* do ask, of course—those constituting the second major stream of criticism mentioned just now. Their questions assume many forms and are presented with different degrees of vehemence but they remain in essentials one question, which asks by what right Robert Penn Warren has transformed Huey Long into Willie Stark. The transformation required an alteration of many of the given facts, and even the suppression of some of the more unsavoury aspects of Long's career, and how can this ever be defended? Their very phrasings of the question suggest their bias, for most of them are firmly convinced that Warren is guilty of irresponsibility or, worse still, of the imaginative equivalent of bad faith. There is an irony to be found here. Most of these commentators see themselves as offering a reply to the formalist school of criticism on *All the King's Men,* raising historical issues which that school prefers to ignore; and yet if to reply can be said to involve the idea of engaging directly with the other side, of achieving some kind of exchange with it, then what they do does not really constitute replying at all. The most that such commentators do is to point out the discrepancies between the facts and the fiction. The possibility of a justification for these discrepancies is hardly raised because, whereas in the case of the formalists the writer is assumed to be isolated from the processes of history, he is here seen to be so immersed in them as to make his proper status that of their recording instrument. The ideal of the poet without any responsibility to history is replaced by the ideal of the scientific historian who has no responsibilities other than this one. The two ideals can hardly engage, being no more than mirror opposites of one another. And the irony is compounded by the fact that this curious state of affairs is ultimately an example of the "terrible division" between philosophical ideal and historical reality which *All the King's Men* exists to demonstrate, the division implicit in the contrast between Willie Stark, the political realist, and Adam Stanton, the naïve man of ideas. This in itself suggests that a minimally acceptable interpretation of the book has to bring the two schools of criticism together, to see what made Warren change history in the way he did and whether his motives, as defined by the structure and purpose of the book, are an adequate justification for his changes. If nothing else, it might indicate to what extent the writer has succeeded in implementing his own recommendations, by squaring his inner needs and beliefs with the "awful responsibility of Time" imposed on him by the outer world of event.

II

Perhaps one way of understanding what Robert Penn Warren has done in *All the King's Men,* as a preparation for assessing his achievement, is to concentrate in the first place on his raw material; that is, the historical facts with which he was presented in the story of Huey Long. Like most stories, Long's is in detail a complicated one, but its main outlines are clear enough. He was born to a poor family in a poor part of the state. At the time of his birth, Louisiana was run by the wealthy planters of the southern counties and the Catholic families who lived in and around New Orleans. The Long family, on the other hand, came from Anglo-Saxon and Protestant stock and had lived for many years in Winn Parish, a county in northern Louisiana which was at once impoverished and powerless. Deprived of a college education, he went to work quite early as a travelling salesman and in the ordinary course of his business acquired a knowledge of, and acquaintanceship with, local tenant-farmers which later proved invaluable. With his earnings, he managed to buy himself time to study for a law degree and then, armed with this, he began to carve out a political career for himself. The mixture of idealism and opportunism which was to become so characteristic of him is suggested by the fact that his favourite reading at this time consisted of radical political pamphlets, and historical or fictional accounts of magnificent demagogues.

Long rose to power with unusual speed even for a southern populist, which is what in a sense he was. He first took political office at the minimum age of twenty-one, and it was only eleven years later, in 1928, that he was elected governor of the state. Once in power, it began to seem unlikely that he could ever be removed. He gradually assumed control of the state legislature, with a mixture of bribery and blackmail, and then so redesigned the political structure of Louisiana as to make almost every public official answerable to him. According to local legend, even the rat-catchers had to prove themselves loyal Huey Long men if they wanted to keep their positions! Whether this legend was true or not, it certainly was true that Long managed to place both the state militia and the highway patrol at his command, and so transform Louisiana into a miniature police state. Elections were rigged, the newspapers were carefully watched and punished with heavy taxes if they proved unusually hostile, and it began to seem that to oppose Huey Long openly in Louisiana was to invite self-destruction.

That is not the whole story, though: if it were, Huey Long would be no more than one in a long line of American demagogues, although perhaps more powerful than most. But the fact is that Long did not just want power as an end in itself. He wanted to use power to implement the kind of schemes which had been his ever since he had been able to think about his situation, and the situation of people like him. He wanted to help the "rednecks" who continued to support him no matter how dictatorial his scheme of government appeared to be. Towards this end, a vast highway system was completed for the state, creating new opportunities for those, usually the poorer classes, trapped until then in the interior. New hospitals and other welfare institutions were opened and, most important of all, universal education was transformed from a theory into a fact when Long made the state rather than the individual responsible for the purchasing of school text-books. The same embryonic socialism characterized his national ambitions. By 1934 he had decided to run for president and, as a preparation for his candidacy, he formulated a "Share Our Wealth" programme of income redistribution which made the "New Deal" look positively conservative. It provided, among other things, for the liquidation of all personal fortunes over three million dollars, generous minimum wages for every American worker white *and* black, a national pension scheme and, in general, close governmental supervision of the economy. Of course, Long's motives in formulating this scheme were practical as well as idealistic: he wanted to appeal to the mass of working-men in the nation just as he had appealed to the poor folk of Louisiana. The scheme cannot be dismissed as simply as that, however, since other American demagogues have proved that there are easier ways of appealing to the popular vote. In the circumstances, to accuse Huey Long of wholesale opportunism would surely be as wrong as to see him as an idealistic man of the people. He was both, in a way, and as such perhaps best defined in terms of the paradox one essentially unsympathetic commentator favoured when he described Huey Long as "a moral idiot of genius."

This is surely the point about Huey Long: that, among those who know or have examined him, even those least sympathetic to his cause have tended to call his story tragic rather than iniquitous. It was the story of a man born into a specific set of historical circumstances which demonstrated to his dissatisfaction that the times were out of joint. In every sense, they denied the demands of his innermost being, what Warren calls "the idea." What he could do in these circumstances seemed fairly clear to him; and can perhaps be defined in terms of what Arthur Koestler, analyzing a similar and more universal situation, described as the alternative attitudes of the Yogi and the Commissar. He could either retreat into himself, and the kind of self-protective narcissism which rejects the world after acknowledging its irremediable iniquity; or he could commit himself to the desperate manoeuvres and partial fulfilments imposed on him by events. In the one case, he would be tending to deny the power which gives life to values; and, in the other, he would be tending to ignore the values which give meaning to power. Long apparently chose the second course. He tried to use corrupt means, in this case the means made available by the political machinery of his state, to achieve his aims; and in the process he could not help corrupting both those aims and himself.

What was true of Huey Long is also true of Willie Stark, no matter how much Warren may alter or condense specific details to make his point. Stark's story is also a tragic one; as tragic and as poignant as, say, that of Brecht's *Mother Courage*. For Willie Stark and Mother Courage are both placed in situations which demand the worst of them, if they are to survive, even though they may recognize and sometimes wish for the best. In this context, scene 3 of *Mother Courage and Her Children* in which the protagonist denies her son, a German soldier, in order to avoid the confiscation of her property by the Swedish army, is comparable to the moment in *All the King's Men* when Willie Stark ruefully accepts the resignation of Hugh Miller, his Attorney-General. Miller, a man of genuine principle, resigns because Stark refuses to prosecute one of his underlings for attempting to divert state funds into his own pocket. Stark *will* punish the man privately but to commit himself to any public form of punishment would be, as he recognizes, to invite political death. His enemies, the people removed from power after the election, have already caught the scent of corruption and are eagerly looking for some concrete evidence to use as a means of pulling the Stark empire down. Willie Stark recognizes what he is doing: he is protecting the unprincipled and denying principle in order to survive. The fact that he wants to stay in power so as to implement his principles only adds a further dimension to the irony and Stark recognizes as much when he says to Miller, just before he leaves, "You're leaving me all alone with the sons-of-bitches. Mine and the other fellow's." The scene epitomizes the entire novel; or at least Willie Stark's part of it. Stark tries to use the powers offered by his given circumstances to realize an idea, but he eventually becomes so involved in the mired complexities of the power game that the idea is forgotten or, worse still, prostituted. And part of the tragedy lies in the fact that Willie Stark senses what is happening to him even while it *is* happening.

What Robert Penn Warren has done in the case of Willie Stark, then, as far as his relationship to his historical prototype is concerned, is to take authenticated facts and reproduce them so as to emphasize their tragic pattern. Certain particulars, such as the nature of the powers assumed by Huey Long in Louisiana and the number and scope of the reforms implemented by him, may be changed: but the paradox which informed the character and life of "the Boss" is not. Perhaps this can be clarified a little more by pointing to one specific example of Warren's treatment of his raw material; and, as in other tragedies, an example more striking than most is supplied by the death of the protagonist. Warren ascribes the death of Willie Stark, with a fine sense of poetic justice, to Dr Adam Stanton; and he accounts for it by suggesting that Adam believed he had been given the directorship of the Willie Stark Hospital in return for favours received by the governor from Anne Stanton, Adam's sister. In fact, Huey Long was shot by one Dr Weiss, who resented the attempts made by the state political machine to deprive his father-in-law, Judge Pavy, of office, and who was even more resentful of remarks made by the governor to the effect that there was black blood in the Pavy family. The differences here between fact and fiction appear to be radical, but they are only apparently so. Long, as one authority on the subject has emphasized, "fell victim . . . to the southern tradition of personal honour and personal violence" when he was killed. His death was precipitated by a characteristic failure to consider the sensibilities of others; and more particularly by his apparent inability to remember just how sensitive southerns can be about the racial taboo, which prohibits an overt acknowledgment of miscegenation. The death of Willie Stark is occasioned by a similar and equally characteristic failure that involves him, although indirectly, in a violation of the *sexual* taboo. Stark takes Anne Stanton, a woman from an old and distinguished Louisiana family, as his mistress, and in the course of their relationship gives her financial help with her orphanages and appoints Adam to be director of his hospital. What he does he does not do as a simple means of rewarding Anne for her services: he is never as crass as that. But there can be no doubt that his generosity towards her is related to his affection for her, and that this affection in turn encourages him to make overtures to Adam Stanton. The offence against the Stanton pride, the smear of prostitution, is implied in the situation and Adam, with his acute sensitivity, merely makes the offence explicit. Perhaps it is not necessary to spell out every detail, though. The point is that the deaths of Huey Long and Willie Stark *are* comparable, in terms of their connexion both with previous mistakes and with a general insensitivity to the narcissistic pride of the idealist. In specifics the two stories may differ: but the tragic pattern of blindness occasioning destruction is the same in either case.

III

To talk about *All the King's Men* in terms only of Willie Stark, however, is to talk about one half of the novel. His story is no more or less important than the story of Jack Burden, the narrator, whose situation throughout most of the narrative is quite the reverse of the protagonist's. Burden is, as he himself acknowledges, an "Idealist" who has adopted the attitude of the Yogi rather than that of the Commissar. He has retreated from the world and from responsibility into that kind of dismissive cynicism which is perhaps the special prerogative of the disillusioned naïf. His characteristic stance, and the reasons for it, are neatly suggested in a passage like the following:

> I'd be lying there in the hole in the middle of my bed where the springs had given down with the weight of wayfaring humanity . . . watching the cigarette smoke flow up and splash against the ceiling . . . like the pale uncertain spirit rising up out of your mouth on the last exhalation, the way the Egyptians figured it, to leave the horizontal tenement of clay in its ill-fitting pants and vest.

What is important about such a passage, I think, is its violent yoking together of heterogeneous ideas, corporeal and spiritual, so as to emphasize their heterogeneity. As Jack Burden sees it, the word can only become flesh by adopting an outfit so ludicrous that it loses all its original character and value; and in these circumstances the best the idealist can do is stand on the side-lines, mocking the world and its squalor. When this in turn becomes intolerable, and the mask of cynicism begins to slip, there is still "the Great Sleep," that retreat into vacuous non-being which is always available to the man of ideas when the world is too much with him.

Jack Burden falls into "the Great Sleep" several times during the course of his life, and the first time is perhaps one of the most significant. This occurs after his abortive attempt at being an historian. Many years ago, Jack explains, he tried to write a dissertation about Cass Mastern, an ancestor who spent most of his life in Kentucky. The facts were compiled over a period of several years and all the details carefully sifted. Burden even went some way towards completing the final draft of the dissertation; and then something happened. Perhaps the later Jack Burden, the man who emerges out of the story of Willie Stark, can describe it best himself:

> Jack Burden could not put down the facts . . . because he did not know Cass Mastern. Jack Burden did not say definitely to himself why he did not know Cass Mastern. But I (who am what Jack Burden became) look back now, years later, and try to say why.
>
> Cass Mastern lived for a few years and in that time he learned that the world is all of one piece. He learned that the world is like an enormous spider web and if you touch it, however lightly, at any one point, the vibration ripples to the remotest perimeter and the drowsy spider feels the tingle and . . . springs out to fling the gossamer coils about you . . . —But how could Jack Burden, being what he was, understand that? . . . to him the world then was simply an accumulation of items, odds and ends of things like the broken and misused and dust-shrouded things gathered in a garret . . . one thing had nothing to do, in the end, with anything else.

What seems to have happened, in effect, was that Burden suddenly found that the dispersed facts in the case of Cass Mastern were assuming shape and significance. The growing coherence of his "items," and the discovery which that coherence was precipitating, were both inviting him to recognize his involvement in history. It was not just that he was being asked to see that he was as implicated in his times and circumstances as Cass Mastern had been in his. This was a part of the offered vision but not all of it. He was also being asked to acknowledge the existence of a *direct* relationship with Cass Mastern, founded on mutual dependence.

That the dependence is mutual is the important point. It is perhaps not difficult to see that, in the context of the interpretation of history which Cass Mastern offers to Jack Burden, the past can be said to shape the present; it is not difficult to see this, and there would probably be few who would disagree with it. What is at once difficult and more interesting, is something that Robert Penn Warren—and eventually Jack Burden—takes to be a corollary of this: that, in a sense, the present can be said to shape the past. The meaning of an event, in other words, is not principally in the event itself but in its complicated relationship with events before and after it. One moment in time interacts with other moments in time. So a pattern is created which is greater than the sum of its parts and which gives an added dimension to each of those parts. This is what Jack Burden cannot see when he is placing "odds and ends" of the past side by side and supposing that, as a result, he is learning the truth about historical experience. He is *not* learning the truth; and he is not simply because he does not realize that what is brought to the past, in terms of the present experience, is at least as important as the separate moment of the past itself.

Such an interpretation of history, which proposes the existence of a dialectical relationship between past and present, is relevant to more of *All the King's Men* than just the story of Jack Burden and Cass Mastern, of course. For it has enormous bearing on the entire structure and meaning of the novel as well. In the first place, it gives the reader a clearer idea of the positive tendencies of the narrative, the alternative to the stances of Yogi and Commissar which is formulated in the course of the action. This alternative is one in which, to quote Warren in another context, values can be said to "grow out of the act of living" and "even as they grow . . . modify living." History, from this standpoint, is neither the set of given and unalterable conditions that Willie Stark takes it to be nor the raw material for the idealistic impulse which Jack Burden would have liked it to be at one time. It is, in a sense, both: a product of the continuing interchange between the human consciousness and his circumstances, past and present. To fail to recognize this is to fall victim to what Burden eventually refers to as "the terrible division of [the] age": to emphasize one term of the dialectic, that is, at the expense of the other. And that the narrator *has* recognized this as a result of the experiences he is now narrating contributes a lot to the extraordinary richness of the book. For, having learnt the truth about historical experience, Jack Burden can discover the meaning of his own story as well as that of Cass Mastern. In *All the King's Men* he is at once describing the sequence of events which led him to know that "the world is all of one piece" and, by reformulating his past in the light of his present recognitions, offering the reader a practical demonstration of his knowledge.

Jack Burden is only the narrator of the book, though. The real teller of the tale is Robert Penn Warren; and this brings us back to the original issue of the relationship between the real Huey Long and the fictional Willie Stark, and the possible point of that relationship. It is surely right to say that, in recasting the story of the legendary "Boss" of Louisiana, Warren is merely doing on a large scale what his narrator does on a slightly smaller one. His revision of history repeats the narrative procedure on another level. For what Warren does is to take the given story, the facts in the case of Huey Long, and set it in the kind of dialectical relationship with an idea that creates a new shape and meaning from both. He does not distort the story, at least in terms of its essential pattern he does not do so. What he does instead is to place it in such a context as will demonstrate its direct and effective relationship with our own experience. The present is changed by the past, in the sense that Warren has found in a specific set of historical circumstances a means of analyzing his own predicament and, as he sees it, the predicament of his "age" as well. And what is more to the point perhaps, the past has been changed by the present since it is only now, in the writing of *All the King's Men,* that the meaning and emphases of the story which Warren recounts become clear. The "odds and ends" of historical memory have been woven into a pattern which makes them "all of one piece" with each other and with the lives of those remembering. Structure in this context becomes a necessary projection of meaning, with the relationship between the writer and the raw material of his tale offering perhaps the most incisive demonstration of those uses of history with which the narrative is concerned. In a way it is a nicely ironic point, which Jack Burden in one of his more sardonic moods might have appreciated, that the reshaping of fact into fiction which so many critics have questioned in *All the King's Men* is really a part of its meaning and formal achievement.

The Case of the Vanishing Narratee: An Inquiry into *All the King's Men*

Simone Vauthier

While the narrator in *All the King's Men* has received much critical attention, his partner in the act of communication has been rather neglected. Yet not only are the two images of narrator and narratee always dependent on each other but in Robert Penn Warren's novel the polarity is all the more marked because, contrary to common usage, the addressee is first to appear on the scene:

> To get there you follow highway 58, going northeast out of the city, and it is a good highway and new. Or was that day we went up it. You look up the highway and it is straight for miles coming at you, black and slick and tarry-shining against the white of the slab . . . and if you don't quit staring at that line and don't take a few deep breaths and slap yourself hard on the back of the neck you'll hypnotize yourself and you'll come to just at the moment when the right front wheel hooks over into the black dirt shoulder off the slab, and you'll try to jerk her back on but you can't because the slab is high like a curb, . . . But you won't make it, course. . . . Then a few days later the boys from the Highway Department will mark the spot with a little metal square painted white and on it in black a skull and crossbones. . . .
>
> But if you wake up in time and don't hook your wheel off the slab, you'll go whipping on into the dazzle. . . .

From *The Southern Literary Journal* 6, no. 2 (Spring 1974). © 1974 by the Department of English, University of North Carolina at Chapel Hill.

> Way off ahead of you, at the horizon where the cottonfields
> are blurred into the light, the slab will glitter and gleam
> like water, as though the road were flooded. You'll go
> whipping toward it, but it will always be ahead of you,
> that bright, flooded place, like a mirage.

And on for two pages before the narrator-agent makes his appearance. Thus it is the narratee who is first made to take the trip to Mason City, to see the hypnotic road and the changing countryside, to face destruction or regeneration through baptismal waters that may be only part of a mirage. The narratee is shocked into awareness of a dangerous future in the extradiegetic world. But unwittingly he has been embarked on the perilous journey of the narration. And the man for whom God's mercy is implored at the end of the second paragraph ("God have mercy on the mariner"), is not simply the man in the car, in "this age of the internal combustion engine," but the man on the road of the narration, the wedding guest suddenly turned mariner, whose precarious voyage through the text this paper proposes to retrace.

The trail of the narratee is not always easy to follow. In the first place the tracks which he leaves in the text are now very broad, now rather faint. Certainly, for long stretches, pronouns may clearly reveal his presence, either the recurrent "you" that proclaims the allocutor, as in the example just quoted, or the occasional "we" that includes the narrator and the receiver as in "we can be quite sure that Hubert had not named the behind guy" or that embraces the interlocutors and the generality of men:

> We get very few of the true images in our heads of the kind
> I am talking about, the kind which becomes more and
> more vivid for us if the passage of the years did not obscure their reality.

Sometimes a change in tenses signals that the orientation of the utterance has changed and become more narrowly focused on the addressee:

> It *was* just the shade of question, of puzzlement.
> But that is something. Not much, but something. It is
> not the left to the jaw and it does not rock them on their
> heels. . . . Nothing lethal, just a moment's pause. But it *is*
> an advantage. *Push* it [italics added].

The passage from narrative to commentary marks the rise of the narratee who is confided in, enlightened, advised, and finally urged to act, with an imperative that introduces him directly in the text. Less obvious still is the network of rhetorical questions that riddles the narration. Sometimes they may be questions which the narrator asks of himself but which might also come from some interlocutor, like the following:

> Judge Irwin had killed Mortimer L. Littlepaugh. But Mortimer had killed Judge Irwin in the end. Or had it been Mortimer? Perhaps I had done it.

The narrator may also be challenging his audience: "A clam has to live, hasn't it?" or taunting his self-pitying narratee: "You bloody fool, do you think you want to milk a cow?" Occasionally, however, the narratee puts his oar in:

> [Jack Burden] might come out and take a drink or take a hand of cards or do any of the other things they did, but what was real was back in that bedroom on the pine table.
>
> What was back in the bedroom on the pine table?
>
> A large packet of letters, eight tattered black bound account books tied together with faded red tape, a photograph.

Needless to say, the narrator knows what is on the table; only a narratee impatient to be told can ask the question from the narrator, who simply relays it. This device is used repeatedly, often as a transition: *What had I read? I had read this.* Some of the narratee's interrogations are not formulated but are revealed by a reiteration of some words or phrases: "Then all at once something happened, and the yellow taste was in the back of my mouth. This happened." Indeed repetitions—a mannerism of the narrator's style—often convey that an impression has to be made on an addressee:

> People still came here for picnics. Well, I had come here for picnics, too. I knew what picnics were like.
>
> I knew what a picnic was, all right.

Explanations also imply an allocutor who must be informed as accurately as possible about what is going on in the diegesis (e.g., "the papers—the administration papers, that is") or in the narration ("I am merely pointing that . . ."). Negations that are in fact assertions suggest that he has to be set right, or reassured: "The fabricator had, on this item, allowed himself the luxury of a little extra material. Not too much. But enough." Many sentences begin with an assertive "no," or "yes," or "oh," and numerous phrases—all right, no doubt, as I say, true, well—answer an implicit remark, objection or question of the addressee. In short, clues to the narratee's presence are abundantly scattered throughout the novel.

Yet, pervasive as it is, this presence remains elusive and after a first reading, one has only a blurred image of the narratee, who, on further investigation, turns out to be a many-sided character. For the sake of brevity, only aspects of the narratee as "you" will be examined here, although other elements of the narration—the questions and pseudo-questions, the intimations and assertions, and the many analogies and comparisons that convey something of the allocutor's habits, attitudes and knowledgeability would also yield precious information. Obviously the addressee of the cited speeches (especially that of Willie's incantatory political speeches) would deserve examination; such a study might throw light on the receiver of the narration but cannot be undertaken here.

The identities of the "you" are so many that some attempt at classification must be made. If we consider the relation of the "you" to the diegesis, we have, at one end of the spectrum, a narratee that is extradiegetic. Such is the case of the "you" that brings the addressee close to the reader. For instance after the narration has depicted at some length Sugar-Boy driving the Governor's Cadillac, the narrator speculates upon the narratee's reaction: "No doubt, you thought Sugar-Boy was a Negro. But he wasn't. He was Irish." Clearly, to entertain such a thought the person addressed must not have been given a sight of Sugar-Boy; he is drawing an incorrect conclusion from his name and therefore he must stand in the position which the reader occupies. More obviously still, the person who is concerned by the remark, "Any act of pure perception is a feat, and if you don't believe it, try it sometime," is challenged to accomplish an action in the extradiegetic world, and may be identified provisionally with the (mock) reader, as is the "you" earnestly advised to "burn his home movies." At the other end of the spectrum, the "you" represents diegetic characters. Theodore and Adam are briefly addressed; Lois is saluted: "Goodbye, Lois, and I forgive you for everything I did to you." A longer passage of the narration is donated to Lucy:

Yes, Lucy, you have to believe that. You have to believe
that to live. I know that you must believe that. And I
would not have you believe otherwise. It must be that
way, and I understand the fact. For you see, Lucy, I must
believe that, too.

Sometimes the "you" refers to Willie Stark:

One time I had wondered why the boss never had the
house painted after he got his front feet in the trough and
a dollar wasn't the reason you got up in the morning any
more.

Sometimes, the "you" is a collective group of anonymous people,
like those who send telegrams of condolence to the governor: "You
couldn't tell that praying [i.e., getting off the telegram] would do
any good, but it certainly never did anybody any harm." A third
position of the narratee as regards the diegesis must be briefly mentioned; in chapter 4, Cass Mastern, being a metadiegetic narrator,
can only have metadiegetic narratees. These include an explicit "you,"
Gilbert, to whom Cass's letters are addressed, and implied narratees
inasmuch as Cass's diary is oriented towards himself ("I write this
down" that "if ever pride is in me, of flesh or spirit, I can peruse
these pages and know with shame what evil has been in me") and
also towards God, in the light of whom the young man tries to judge
his life, and who is once directly addressed, "O God and my Redeemer!"

The appearances of the purely diegetic and extradiegetic narratees
are few and far between in comparison with those of yet another
category to be studied next. But with the exception of the
metadiegetic narratee, restricted to the confines of chapter 4, they are
distributed fairly regularly throughout the novel. And significantly
the appeal to a diegetic "you" that is at once most developed in terms
of the utterance and most significant in terms of the theme, namely
that to Lucy, is placed towards the end. Worthy of notice, too, a
"you" is made to represent Willie only in the chapters describing his
early career. Although *comparatively* little represented, these categories are important insofar as they project a full range of positions and
by setting up a number of secondary narratees, to whom the narration is only addressed occasionally, increase the complexity of the
"implied dialogue" which, as Wayne Booth has observed [in *The*

Rhetoric of Fiction], goes on among author, narrator, the other characters; the reader, and it must be added, the narratees.

Furthermore, since, as narrator-participant the "I" has a dual nature, so has the narratee; the duality is evidenced in the report of Willie's rhetorical power over listening crowds: "I would wait for the roar. You *can't help it*. I knew it would come, but I would wait for it" (italics added). In his case the "you" includes both a diegetic character—the experiencing self—and an extradiegetic person—the narrating self distancing himself from Jack Burden the participant— plus an undetermined someone, also extradiegetic—any man in the same kind of situation. Or take the passage, too long to be quoted here, when Jack muses on "the Friend of Your Youth [who] is the only friend you will ever have, for he does not see you." The "you" designates again an undetermined man, who can bear any name, "Spike, Bud, Snip, Red, Rusty, Jack, Dave," exemplifying a common human experience. But the "you" addressed at the end of the mediation is so close to the experiencing self that he is then called Jack: The Friend of Your Youth "speaks your name . . . saying, 'Well, Jack, damned glad you came, come on in, boy!' " The time flow of the narrative was interrupted, as Adam Stanton came to the door to greet Jack, for a disquisition on "The Friend of Your Youth"; we then are smoothly let back into the narrative by the reduction of the "you" to one of its components, the narrator, who now hears the words his friend has been speaking. Moreover many occurrences of the second person belong to the level of the enunciation rather than to that of the diegesis, introduced as they are in the images brought up by the locutor (e.g., "[I could] let all the pictures of things a man might want run through my head . . . and let them all slide off, like a deck of cars slewing slowly off your hand. Maybe the things you want are like cards.")

Confronted therefore with a multiplicity of "you's" the reader finds himself trying to assess the referential extension of specific instances, wondering how big or limited is such and such a "you." In some cases, the second person is, so to say, all-inclusive:

> After a great blow, or crisis, after the first shock and then
> after the nerves have stopped screaming and twitching,
> you settle down to the new condition of things.

This we may call, in parody of Jack Burden, The Aphoristic You. (Of course, the Aphoristic You can only embody the wisdom of mankind as filtered through the unconscious assumptions of the narrator.) A more limited but still fairly extensive "you" is the Mythical American:

> For that is where you come, after you have crossed oceans and eaten stale biscuits while prisoned forty days and nights in a stormy-tossed rat-trap, after you have sweated in the greenery and heard the savage whoop, after you have built cabins and cities and bridged rivers, after you have lain with women and scattered children like millet seed in a high wind, after you have composed resonant documents, made noble speeches, and bathed your arms in blood to the elbows, after you have shaken with malaria in the marshes and in the icy wind across the high plains. This is where you come to lie alone in a bed in a hotel room in Long Beach, California. Where I lay."

We have here the Archetypical American Hero, already described though less ambiguously, by Tocqueville, and epitomizing American history. In another version, the historical archetype is resolved into distinct roles—murderer, gold-rusher, Greeley's young man, etc.—which reveal more clearly the American nightmare along with the American dream.

> For West is where we all plan to go some day. It is where you go when the land gives out and the oldfield pines encroach. It is where you go when you get the letter saying: *Flee, all is discovered.* It is where you go when you look down at the blade in your hand and see the blood on it. It is where you go when you are told that you are a bubble on the tide of empire. It is where you go when you hear that there's gold in them-thar hills. It is where you go to grow up with the country. It is where you go to spend your old age. Or it is just where you go.

The Mythical American is easily reduced into the Average American: "When you don't like it where you are, you always go west." Indeed the Average American and his experiences are often invoked. On occasion he is even provided with a family:

> It was like a showing of a family movie, the kind the advertisements tell you to keep so that you will have a record of the day Susie took her first little toddle and the

> day Johnny went off to kindergarten and the day you went
> up Pike's Peak and the day of the picnic on the old home
> farm and the day you were made chief sales manager and
> bought your first Buick.

Little Susie reappears at least twice as the average child of the Average American, *you*. Occasionally, the Average American turns Southerner: "You don't get rich being an Attorney General in a Southern State." Clearly determined by the narrative situation in the case of the Attentive Observer, who has the opportunity to watch the characters in action, although sometimes the observer is only the Virtual Observer: "the atmosphere would have reminded you of a morgue." Determined and yet indefinite is the Equivocal Participant, the "you" that "represents" both a diegetic character and an allocutor *persona,* singular or plural:

> The gentlemen from the city persuaded Willie that he was
> the savior of the state. I suppose that Willie had his natural
> quota of ordinary suspicion and cageyness, but those things
> tend to evaporate when what people tell you is what you
> want to hear.

A particular variety of the Equivocal Participant, the Disguised Narrator, is a recurrent figure: the above-mentioned passage on the Friend of Your Youth furnishes a typical example. Hesitation as to the identity of the Disguised Narrator is possible because somehow our expectancy is not answered. For instance we naturally expect the "you" in the following sentence to encompass the allocuter:

> For after the dream there is no reason why you should not
> go back and face the fact which you have fled from (even
> if the fact seems to be that you have, by digging the truth
> about the past, handed over Anne Stanton to Willie Stark),
> for any place to which you may flee will not be like the
> place from which you have fled, and you might as well go
> back, after all, to the place where you belong, for nothing
> was your fault or anybody's fault for things are always as
> they are.

But although in the main sentence the second-person generalizes and covers a multitude of experiences, on which the immediate context and the many allusions to the myth of the West throw light, we realize with something of a jolt that the "you" in the parenthesis can only refer to Jack Burden, since he alone can have done the particular action mentioned. Then the other "you's" of the passage are felt as representing the narrator.

But such examples also provide us with a clue to the functioning of the second-person. Often it is made to stand for the first-person in a figure that can be called *speaker/addressee* (*destinateur/destinataire*) *commutation*. In *All the King's Men* commutation of the interlocutors is a systematic device which deserves closer scrutiny.

Destinateur/destinataire commutation is by far the most frequent. Avowedly the story of Willie's rise from "Cousin Willie" to Governor Stark, the narration is therefore apparently oriented towards outsiders who have some knowledge of the Boss's career, without being in possession of all the facts and, above all, of the meaning of them. But even before the narrator discloses personal information about himself, long before he owns that this "is [his] story, too," Jack Burden betrays the autobiographic nature of his narrative when he makes the "you" a reflection of his self, and the outside allocutor an inner auditor. Amusingly enough, this is symbolized in one minor detail: when Willie exerts his oratorical spell on the Mason City crowd, "you could hear one insane and irrelevant July fly sawing away up in one of the catalpa trees." If here the "you" can represent the anonymous listeners, in the following repetition of the notation, the "you" can no longer do so and the present tense underlines that the sensation is one of the narrator's: "there was only the sound of the July flies, which *seems* to be inside your head as though it were the grind and whir of the springs and cogs which are you."

But when the narrator declares "I have a story. It is the story of a man who lived in the world and the world looked one way for a long time" and then goes on to summarize his evolution in third-person terms for three paragraphs, he uses a *terminal/non-terminal commutation* to put some distance between his past self and the re-generated self, which, however, is grammatically and dramatically reborn at the end of the last paragraph: "It looks as though Hugh will get back into politics and when he does I'll be along to hold his coat." And reborn, too, complete with a past still active in the present as indicated by the tense: "*I've had* some valuable experience in that line" (italics added). Seeing Willie for the first time, Jack Burden is, unknowingly, meeting fate, so this is how the narrator reports the occasion:

> Metaphysically it was the Boss, but how was I to know? Fate comes walking through the door and it is five feet eleven inches tall and heavyish in the chest and shortish in the leg and is wearing a seven-fifty seersucker suit . . . and a stiff high collar like a Sunday-school superintendent and a blue-striped tie which you know his wife gave him last Christmas and which he has kept in tissue paper with the holly card ("Merry Christmas to my Darling Willie from your Loving Wife") until he got ready to go to the city, and a gray felt hat with the sweat stains showing through the band. It comes in just like that and how are you to know? It comes in, trailing behind Alex Michel.

In the whole paragraph, Willie is referred to by an apersonal pronoun, except in the relative clause which deals with his personal life, symbolized by the Christmas *tie* and represented by a new correlation *my–your,* where, incidentally, one expects *his*. However, when after the introduction of Willie as husband the narration returns to Willie as the embodiment of Fate, not only is the apersonal "it" resumed, for an effect which is now more marked than in the first occurrence from being pointedly repeated; but with the repetition of the transformed question and the use of "you," (how are you to know?), both narrator and narratee are made responsible for the *person/nonperson commutation,* which betrays their common unawareness of Willie's potentialities and of the mysterious ways of fate. *Definite/indefinite commutations* are also to be found (e.g., "*They* called that Idealism in *my* book I had when I was in college," italics added). But since such turns are common enough in everyday speech they need not be emphasized. An arresting sentence may be mentioned here:

> In a hanging you do not change a man's personality. You just change the length of his neck and give him a quizzical expression, and in an electrocution you just cook some bouncing meat in a wholesale lot.

One would rather expect something like: a man's personality is not changed, and only the length of his neck is changed, clauses that would leave the responsibility for these drastic measures unassigned, whereas the "you" involves the allocutor in the executioner's role or in society's meting out of punishment.

Apart from commutations—the substitution of one person (or nonperson) for another on the paradigmatic axis of the narration—permutations—a substitution on the syntagmatic axis—also play prominent part in *All the King's Men*. In chapter 4, the narrating self assumes toward a period of his own life, with a measure of self-parody, the detached stance which the acting self took as history graduate toward Cass Mastern, the object of his research. The first-person narrator then turns into a third-person character, "Jack Burden" and "he," while Cass, a third person in the diegetic narration, now becomes a speaking "I," whose letters and journal are abundantly cited. As a consequence of this permutation, the "you" of the overall narrative situation can become a "we."

> [The journal] did not report what book it was that Gilbert's riding crop tapped. It is not important what book it was. Or perhaps it is important, for something in *our* mind, in *our* imagination wants to know that fact. *We see* the red, square, strong hand ("my brother is strong made and florid") protruding from the white cuff, grasping the crop which in that grasp looks fragile like a twig. *We see* the flick of the little leather loop on the page, a flick brisk, not quite contemptuous, but *we cannot* make out the page [italics added].

Here the first-person plural, while it excludes the first-person singular subject of the embedded utterance, includes four kinds of participants in the act of communication—the implied author whose fairly discrete presence in the sequence is here made manifest, "Jack Burden," the narratee(s), and the reader; all four stand on almost equal footing in respect to the fact under scrutiny since to all of them (or us) it is something out of the past, fictive or real, which has to be deciphered. Obviously the "I" of the diegetic story can never say "we," meaning himself and his narratee and/or reader, when he tells or ponders about acts of his own life, but only when he speculates or moralizes on the human condition. (And as a matter of fact there are a few such cases of a universal "we.") He could, of course, write, "We wonder what books Cousin Willie read in the lonely, cold upstairs room." But this would shape a different relation between narrator and narratee from that which is firmly established from the opening sentence of the novel and the narrator never uses the first-person plural to puzzle out the enigma that is Willie Stark.

Commutations and permutations, as might be expected, often interact, creating complex moves across the narrational chessboard.

> (1) At night you pass through a little town where you once lived, and you expect to see yourself wearing knee pants, standing all alone on the street corner under the hanging bulbs. . . . (2) You expect to see that boy standing there under the street lamp, out too late, and you feel like telling him to go to bed or there will be hell to pay. (3) But maybe you are at home in bed and sound asleep and not dreaming and nothing has ever happened that seems to have happened. (4) But, then, who the hell is this in the back seat of the big black Cadillac that comes ghosting through the town? (5) Why, this is Jack Burden. Don't you remember little Jack Burden? He used to go out in his boat in the afternoon on the bay to fish, and come home and eat his supper and kiss his beautiful mother goodnight and say his prayers and go to bed at nine-thirty. (6) Oh, you mean old Ellis Burden's boy? (7) Yeah, and that woman he married out of Texas—or was it Arkansas?—that big-eyed, thin-faced woman who lives up there in that old Burden place now with that man she got herself. Whatever happened to Ellis Burden? Hell, I don't know, nobody around here had any word going on years. He was a queer 'un. Damn if he wasn't queer, going off and leaving a real looker like that woman out of Arkansas. Maybe he couldn't give her what she craved. Well, he gave her that boy, that Jack Burden. Yeah.
>
> You come into the town at night and there are the voices.

In the first sentence, we may take the "you" to be the narratee (n) and a projection of the narrator (N) who has just been telling about such a ride to Burden's Landing; "yourself wearing knee pants" is a reduction in time of $N+n$, a past self of both narrator and narratee. But his past self takes on an independent life and becomes a third person, *that boy, he*, in sentence (2). The "you" of sentence (3) seems to be $N+n$ again, with the difference, however, that n seems to have dwindled in size: the first narratee could be almost any reader of the male sex with a smalltown background; whereas now the possibility that the narratee could also be the reader is more radically excluded since n is perhaps asleep—which the reader of *All the King's Men* cannot be, of course. With the question of sentence (4) a *voice* is heard, which, as the answer makes clear, implies a speaking "I." However, this "I" cannot be the first-person narrator since *he* is now ensconced in the text as the referent of the query, the man in the back seat of the Cadillac. The voice can only be the voice of n. Nor is the transformation of $N+n$ complete inasmuch as n further splits into two dialoguing characters, one who recognizes "little Jack Burden" (n_1) and one (n_2) who has to be reminded of the identity (through blood kin, a misleading index) of Jack Burden. By now neither can be considered indefinite, extradiegetic addressees. Absorbed into the story, they also become active participants in the narration as they take over the narrating role, providing the reader with new information on Jack Burden's background. The permutation is complete when the knowledgeable n_1 uses the first-person "Hell, *I* don't know." Yet this is an empty "I," whose outlines will never be filled and whose sole function is to displace the narrating self, who could have given us this kind of information, and thus modify the addressee, an effect which is enhanced by the fact that the typography—the absence of commas, the juxtaposition of question and answer—makes it impossible at the end of the dialogue to discriminate with certainty between the two interlocutors.

Another interesting transformation of the "you" can be observed in the following passage.

> (1) Which is nonsense, for whatever you live is Life. (2) That is something to remember when you meet the old classmate who says, "Well, now, on our last expedition up the Congo—" or the one who says, "Gee, I got the sweetest little wife and three of the swellest kids ever—" (3) You must remember it when you sit in hotel lobbies, or lean over bars to talk to the bartender, or stand in a dark street at night, in early March, and stare into a lighted window. (4) And remember little Susie in there has adenoids and the bread is probably burned, and turn up the street, for the time has come to hand me down that walking cane, for I got to catch that midnight train, for all my sin is taken away. For whatever you live is Life.

After comprehending $N + n + n + n \ldots$ in sentence (1), the extension of the "you" progressively diminishes until in the last part of sentence (3) it coincides with N, the narrator who happened to be staring into a lighted window on an early March night when he went into this philosophical mood. Yet with sentence (4) and the imperative *remember,* which modulates the earlier *it is something to remember,* followed by *you must remember,* the "you" designates a definite singular *n;* only, in this case, the narratee is revealed as an alter ego of the narrator, who then reappears as "me" and then "I." But, although defined through grammatical marks and through the situation (Jack Burden is on his way to catch the night train to Memphis and to uncover Judge Irwin's guilty secret), the "I" is in fact more—therefore less—than Jack Burden's self: it is the indefinite "I" of the popular song, the blues and the spiritual, as phrasing and rhythm connote, so that it can easily become again the generalizing, aphoristic "You" at the end of the paragraph: Whatever you/one/man live[s] is Life. In short, the narratee is a Protean figure who alternately dilates and contracts and keeps changing positions in the narration, with the result that the distance separating it from the other figures increases or decreases accordingly, and the pattern of relationships between them shifts like a kaleidoscope.

Throughout all this, the characteristic feature of the narratee is his dependence on the narrator. Even at the farthest distance—as fictive reader—the "you" is dependent for his very existence on the "I" that projects him as an image of the Other. And this Other, notwithstanding his more checquered career (as outlaw or family man, for instance) is not very different from the experiencing self. The composite narratee has participated in some of Jack's experiences, been subjected to the fascination of Willie, seen Anne Stanton as a young girl, taken the meaningful trip to the West, and has had, in a word, an American education. Although he may be unaware of certain aspects of the South, since things have to be described to him, he is still very familiar with southern life as many analogies show, and he knows for example what it feels like to have "a sizable chunk of dry cornpone stuck in [his] throat." A man of culture, he can pick up allusions to Prometheus or echoes of Poe in the wind that "didn't chill us or kill us in the kingdom by the sea." More significantly, the narratee has Jack Burden's inquisitive mind—witness all the passages developed through questions—and he shares in his basic assumptions on life as evinced in the many generalizations. Thus he reveals Jack's need to extract private meaning out of public events and to socialize personal meaning in a dialectic process. (To this extent, the frequent use and the nature of the adjunctive "you" partly reflects and shapes

Jack's attempts to "re-establish his values within a different social framework" from that of Burden's Landing.) Even in his talents as a quick-change artist, the addressee mirrors the narrator, a self-confessed *Svengali*. Thus in his choice of narratees, Jack Burden betrays both his anxiety at being limited, defined, limited *because* defined, and his desire for self-definition.

For to turn to the Other is to meet the Self, but to face the Self is to encounter the Other. *Je est un autre.* And in *All the King's Men,* the "you" is an *alter* ego—not a past vanished self, however, to whom the narrator would talk across the gap of years, in the typical autobiographical stance. (Needless to say there is such a distance in time and identity between the narrating and the acting selves, but it is marked through a number of elements, temporal adverbs, tenses, whole comments [*that was what I thought I had learned*] and an episodic use of the third person, etc.—which cannot be studied here.) On the contrary, the "you" would seem to speak for a "not-dead" self since he relives in an intemporal, almost dream-like present some of the experiences of Jack.

> But as the train pulls away, a woman comes to the back door of one of the houses—just the figure of a woman for you cannot make out the face. . . . She goes back into the house. To what is in the house . . . but you cannot see the walls to the secret to which the woman has gone in.
>
> The train pulls away, faster now and the woman is back in the house where she is going to stay. She'll stay there. And all at once, you think that you are the one who is running away and who had better run fast to wherever you are going for it will be dark soon . . .
>
> But nothing happens, and you remember that the woman had not even looked up at the train. You forget her, and the train goes fast, and is going fast when it crosses a little trestle. . . . [You] see the cow standing in the water upstream near the single leaning willow. And all at once you feel like crying. But the train is going fast, and almost whatever you feel is taken away from you, too.
>
> You bloody fool, do you think that you want to milk a cow?
>
> You do not want to milk a cow.
>
> Then you are at Upton.

Against the increasing speed of the train, (although it moves through "cloying," "syrup"-like air), is balanced the stagnancy of the "you," the self becalmed in the treacly waters of an eternal present, unable to detach himself from the images and feelings which Jack believes have been taken away from him but which "stay there" forever. And surely, the woman appearing only to disappear, going back to her secret behind the walls, and even the cow with her milk now forever unavailable remain there in the narrator's *speech* because their verbal evocation reanimates older images, older feelings—the longing for a mother's love, the desire to know the secret behind the parents' door. (This is, however, a privileged example, insofar as the metonymical chain of desire is short and the repressed material can be perceived through the actual images.) But it would be absurd to say that the disjunctive "you" is Jack Burden's unconscious self. Rather when he addresses this "you," the narrator projects a split state of consciousness. Nor can this "you" be called Jack's "bad" self, for he is as guilty as but no guiltier than the "I." In fact, he is a *double* whose raison d'être seems to be his non-subjectivity. Jack Burden suffers from a sense of unreality which makes him see others as unreal too: "Oh, they are real, all right, and it may be the reason they don't seem real to you is that you aren't very real yourself." Unable to see himself clearly, he posits in the disjunctive "you" the double that embodies him, that makes *him* visible because *he* can address it. *Percipi est esse,* and to speak is to make oneself perceived.

Therefore, if the polarity of "you" and "I" points to the disassociation of Jack Burden's personality, what can hold Jack-as-Humpty-Dumpty together is precisely the hyphen of the interlocutory act. Furthermore the disjunctive "you" performs its part in the act so satisfactorily that it is truly a "didactic you." By in fact telling parts of his story—the trip to Mason City, the trip to Burden's Landing, the trip to Upton, in particular—through a second person, the first-person narrator shows that he is not yet fully aware of all the aspects of his own life or is at any rate reluctant to face them. The "you" which conveniently separates and distances experience also clarifies it, and assumes the function which Michel Butor assigns to the second person, marking "a progress in self-consciousness, the very birth of language, or of *a* language." Indirect confirmation can be found in the Cass Mastern episode. Cass, who is convinced of his personal guilt and can explain his sinfulness in theological terms, simply records his testimony through a straightforward first-person narration, although he is aware that his present "I" is different from his past "I." So "you" is a form of address which, with but one exception, he reserves for a "real" allocutor and whenever he wants to generalize he uses apersonal forms (such as *it is dishonorable to spy upon another*) or the indefinite *man* (*Man is never safe*) and "one" (*One can only know oneself in God*). Direct confirmation is brought by the gradual disappearance of the disjunctive "you" in Jack Burden's speech. Already the last chapter contains noticeably fewer occurrences and there are none after the visit to Lucy, which marks a high point in Jack's acceptance of Willie Stark and of himself.

From the beginning, in any case, balancing the egocentrism and disintegration of a self refracted in a multiplicity of "you"s there is the structure that both shapes and expresses the relation of Jack to the world. Despite all temptations to disengage himself, to retreat to the solitude of the anonymous room in Long Beach or, more drastically, into the Great Sleep, Jack also needs to establish relationships with an Other. Thus, in his relation, discourse, "a statement presupposing a locutor and an auditor, and in the first named an intention of influencing the second in some way" predominates over "récit," a "narrative of past events." Although passages from the former type of utterance to the latter and back are frequent, *All the King's Men* is overwhelmingly a discourse. Consequently, it is difficult to agree entirely with Franz Stanzel's statement that

> the first-person narrator's eccentric position is the reason why long stretches of the novel contain no real first-person references. . . . From a given page of such a section it is often impossible to decide whether the work is a first-person novel or a third-person novel.
>
> (*Narrative Situations in the Novel*)

Although the narrator may not be present, he is represented in the text often through his faithful companion, the narratee. See, for instance, the many signs of the latter in the description of Willie's early career, which the narrator reconstructs. The permanence of the addressee, whether the disjunctive "you," the adjunctive "you," or the truly nonsubjective person, testifies to the protagonist's deep need for relatedness. Besides, the narratee does not usually condescend to his allocutor, although he may be something of an authoritarian, enjoining behavior (*you ride*) or ideas (*you think*). On occasion too he may give him a piece of advice: "If you ask something quick and sharp out of a clear sky you may get an answer you never would get otherwise." But insofar as the narratee is often made, through comments and analogies, to carry part of the ideological burden of the novel, his experience is necessarily considered to be as valid as that of the narrator.

This points to another of the many functions of the narratee. He does not simply contribute to the characterization of the narrator but plays a part in the elaboration of the ideas and themes of the novel. In the generalizations and similes, the adjunctive "you" provides the clarifying parallel and guarantees the general application of whatever Jack may feel or think. Making the story more natural, the narratee also makes its ideological message more acceptable, because apparently accepted within the textual dialogue. To him, indeed, is delegated one of the functions which Robert Penn Warren assigned to his narrator, that of chorus, for which it is better suited than Jack Burden, being collective, anonymous, and already aware of the public aspects of the drama whose hidden patterns Burden is seeking to trace out. Because it is changeable and unobtrusive, this chorus does not harden temporary half-truths into eternal verities, thus preserving the dialectic complexity of the novel. Because it is undefined, it can enhance both the American dimension of the action and the "tragedy of incomplete personalities"—which, beyond the southern or American affabulation, is the real theme of the work.

The relation of narratee and theme is even more interesting. For one thing, if in *All the King's Men,* "a plurality of heroes is one symbol of a riven world," so is a multiplicity of narratees a further symbol of a riven self in a riven world, as the contrast between Jack Burden's narration and Cass Mastern's emphasizes. Yet regeneration, rebirth, in other words a newer integration, remains possible, partly because through language can be discovered anew the "complicity of relatedness." Moreover, although identity, contrary to what some of the characters may believe, is not fixed and unchanging, man is nonetheless responsible for his actions—a lesson for which Jack pays with "blood." While the Protean "you" becomes the mask of an uncertain, shifting self, the pronominal permanence of the "I"—despite a few eclipses—asserts the continuity of moral responsibility, notwithstanding. Conversely the persistence of the "yous" in the part of the narration concerned with the *discovery* of meaning affirms again that self-realization depends on the realization of the

Other. Thus the autobiographical narration can be both the recognition and the acting-out of man's accountability.

If we go into the functioning of the text, the complex moves of the interlocutors, the permutations and commutations mirror the central metaphor of the novel, the image of the web. Just as "the world is all of one piece," so is speech: if you touch the "web of things" and the web of words—"however lightly, at any point," "the vibrations ripple to the remotest perimeter." With every change of addressee, the narrator sends ripples that modify not only the arrangement of the verbal parts of his utterance but his relations to the allocutor, to the message and hence to the world. These substitutions also undercut the antimony of the "I" and the "you," the ego and the non-ego, the self and the world, which are then seen to be dialectically generating one another. "Direction is all."

In addition, the chess-like moves of the interlocutory figures may also serve to modalize the narrator's conscious attitudes. Alone in his car, Jack finds comfort in a sense of depersonalization:

> They say you are not you, except in terms of relation to other people. If there weren't any other people there wouldn't be any you because what you do, which is what you are, only has meaning in relation to other people. That is a very comforting thought when you are in the car in the rain at night alone, for then you aren't you, and not being you or anything, you can really lie back and get some rest. It is a vacation from being you.

By the use of the introductory "*they* say," and of the conditional tense, as well as by the flippancy of his tone in the rest of the passage, Burden seems to discount the theory even as he expounds it—a characteristic stance of Jack, who likes to have his cake and eat it. But the text yet hints at a different story. The "I" installs an insistent "you" in place of itself, thus suggesting intersubjectivity and the inversibility of "I" and "you." This seemingly bears out the idea that you are not you except in the presence of people. At the same time, it suggests that the idea is acceptable only at a certain level. Even in solitude the "I" can posit a "you" to relate to, in the socialized structure of language. Jack Burden, indeed, manipulates language so resourcefully that he convinces us that man, the speaking animal, can never be really alone: language provides him with a built-in allocutor.

No wonder then that the relationship of narrator and narratee shapes the process of self-knowledge which is the protagonist's central experience. At the beginning of his narration which not only tells about but mirrors his quest, Jack Burden who has little sense of identity, confronts himself with a series of nararatees, who, whether imaginary or "real," represent faces of the self he is looking for. He commits what Cass Mastern, who lived in a world where men were more complete, less scattered and could relate more easily to a transcendence, considers a human error, the error of trying "to know oneself by the self of another" instead of in "God's eye." In "the age of the internal combustion engine," however, it would seem to be less a defect than a normal pattern of behavior. And the protagonist achieves maturity through what Robert Penn Warren calls elsewhere an "osmosis of being which in the end does not deny, but affirms his identity." With its use of narratees, its permutations and commutations, its disjunctive and adjunctive "you"s that overlap and may fade out into one another, the narration embodies the process of interpenetration and of readjustment of perspectives. Through the shifting patterns of relations, "new perspectives" and "new values" are being created and Jack comes to discover his kinship with other men, i.e., his participation in human guilt at the same time as he realizes his unavoidable isolation. Hence, as has been pointed out, the need for the disjunctive "you" reflecting the split self and for the adjunctive "you" mirroring the defining Other diminishes.

As Jack's quest for identity passes through tentative and incomplete identifications with father figures that he in a sense kills, for "the truth always kills the father," so does his struggle for integration pass through incomplete cleavage of the self, for "separateness is identity." And he can get rid of the obsessive inner narratee when, having been reborn, he is at last able to tell his version of the "family romance" to Anne Stanton: "I had to tell it to somebody," he says to Anne, "I had to say it out loud—to be sure it's true [that he is changed]. But it is true. . . . It's my mother, you know." Jack can now tell the significant encounter with his mother and the return to Anne without any mediation. Similarly, the next-to-last generalization of the novel is one that stresses no longer the interrelatedness of the subjective to the nonsubjective but the relation between the one and the many, the individual and mankind. "For *each of us* is the son of a million fathers." No doubt as he goes out into "the convulsion of the world," Jack Burden will be involved in new patterns of relationships. No doubt the self-knowledge he has acquired is incomplete but he has achieved an awareness that enables him to stand alone and yet say "we," whether the "we" includes only his wife, or all of us, the children of a million fathers. Having told his story the narrator can make a *new* beginning and, turning historian, write the formerly abandoned life of Cass Mastern whom he "now may come to understand." And in the Life, *récit* ought to prevail over discourse, narrative over narration, in conformity with a scholarly code that Burden can now accept because he has found his true language.

In short, the narratee has become expendable. And his fate also concerns the reader. True, reader and narratee are not to be confused. But by the same polarity that creates the dependence of the narrative "you" and the narrative "I," the reversibility of "you" and "I" works not only within the story-telling situation but, to some degree, within the reading situation. I, the reader, cannot help feeling somehow implied in the "you" that is being addressed so insistently, even as I realize that this is a doubly fictive you with a fictive experience which may be quite remote from mine. The brilliant introduction that whizzes the narratee over the road to Mason City and the "great mirage" of the meaning of the novel may help set up the reader's partial identification with the narratee before he has had the opportunity to begin establishing the more usual identification with the protagonist and perhaps it brings him thus closer to the authorial *persona*. In any case, the reader is perforce implicated in the experience of the narratee, if only to the extent that he has to strip off his masks, and keep track of who and where he is. Thus the transformations of the narratee upset the reader's facile certainties and engage him in a quest of his own which parallels that of the narrator. Should he refuse to identify provisionally with the protagonist and to share in his burden of human guilt, he is jolted into awareness of his guilt as virtual narratee, whether the latter is cast in the role of conventional brigand or less conventional executioner. "L'hypocrite lecteur, mon semblable, mon frère" must acknowledge himself an accomplice of either the acting self, or the narrator, or the narratee—if not of all three of them. But he is thereby offered the chance—together with the advice—to "be baptized to be born again," too. Redemption is available to every reader willing to change, to "burn his home movies," to accept his commitment as reader and play the metonymic and metaphoric game of the novel.

Yet woe to the unwary reader who has accepted in good faith the role of next of kin to the narratee. When the regenerated "I" throws overboard the now useless "you," he may feel like a cast-away, may at least experience a sense of depletion. Having been allowed the freedom of many squares across the board, he now discovers that his moves are severely restricted, and few positions open to him from which to view the narrator's "picture of the world." But he had had his warning in the introduction with its recurrent images of car-wrecks and the perils of water. So he too is, in a sense, back at the beginning, as Jack Burden is back at his dissertation grappling with the task of understanding Cass Mastern and relating his story. The task for the reader is to start assessing anew the characters' half-truths (Cass Mastern's and Willie Stark's and Jack Burden's) in the light of the whole truth. But the whole truth, of course, can, in this case, only be that embodied in the novel, a "myth" of "human nature's trying to fulfill itself," Humpty-Dumpty poised back on his wall by the grace of *All the King's Men*. To that extent too, it is a form in which the reader collaborates in the dialectical process of reading, and for which he must therefore assume some responsibility. God have mercy on all reading mariners.

"The Case of the Upright Judge": The Nature of Truth in *All the King's Men*

Richard G. Law

Though controversies concerning Robert Penn Warren's most successful novel still occasionally emerge, it is generally agreed that *All the King's Men* is an elaborate "parable of fact and truth." The moral or ethical terms in which this parable is worked out have been fully and intelligently described by critics; Jack Burden's struggle for self-definition, the large, underlying mythical movement of flight from reality (or "separateness") and eventual and painful return to acceptance, responsibility, and a sense of community are as well defined as most things in literary criticism can be. Behind these ethical terms, however, lies another dimension, another elaborate parable which has to do, simply, with the way the mind orients itself in the incomprehensible flux of the world and creates in it some sustaining order and meaning. In addition, this parable of the nature of human knowledge and perception is bound up with the aesthetic assumptions which Warren has explored throughout his career in every genre he has touched. Both the epistemological and aesthetic ideas are, like the ethical issues, embodied in the structure of the novel; they are implicit in the very manner of its unfolding.

"Duplicity" and "doubleness" are key words in Warren's description of experience and nowhere in his work does the structure of a novel better imitate the doubleness of experience, the dual structure or "dialectical configurations" of "truth" itself, than in *All the King's Men*. On the most basic level, the novel has, rather than a single

From *Studies in American Fiction* 6, no. 1 (Spring 1978). © 1978 by Northeastern University.

center of interest, two counterpointed plot lines: Willie Stark's political career and Jack Burden's struggle for understanding. With the
intrusion of Burden's consciousness into the action of the Stark story,
Warren turns the decline and fall of a great man and public figure into
a bildungsroman, a story of the education of a young man and his
initiation into the world. The Jack Burden who attempts to tell the
story of Willie Stark and who tells his own in the process belongs to
a long tradition of observer-narrators whose function is to demonstrate the deceptiveness and subjectivity of experience: Lambert
Strether, Miles Coverdale, Nick Carraway, and Conrad's Marlow
are Burden's cousins and antecedents. These two plot lines are,
moreover, different in emphasis as well as in content and create a
curious double perspective, a stereopticon effect (to borrow one of
Warren's favorite images). Readers primarily interested in the Stark
plot have often praised the sense of history in the novel, the careful
documentation, the "facts" so laboriously and objectively set forth,
as if Warren, in spite of his disclaimers, had attempted a biography
of Huey Long. But one need only remember the mode of narration
and the unreliability of Burden as narrator to recall how purely subjective the apparently "historical" account is. What Burden sees is
always a function of what an event means to him at a given time, and
his hard "facts" have a way of altering in the course of the book as
Jack himself changes. This structuring device is one reflection of the
often-mentioned dichotomy of "facts" and "value," or "facts" and
"truth," which pervades the novel. The terms imply, among other
things, two modes of perception: one rational, objective, and quan-
titative (the mode characteristic of a "scientific society"), and the
other intuitive, subjective, and qualitative. In other words, even at
this level, the structure of the novel embodies and dramatizes its
themes.

Warren's use of the terms also places him in a specific artistic and
philosophical tradition of Humanist protest against the doctrine of
scientific materialism, the belief that only what can be measured is
real. While hostility toward such a view ("scientism" as the Nashville Agrarians called it) has been widespread among artists from the
nineteenth century on, Warren has been unusually, almost obses-
sively, preoccupied with the issue. Both in his concern and in his
intellectual grasp of the problem, Warren is very clearly the student
of John Crowe Ransom. Ransom, the most systematic thinker among
the Nashville group, had studied under F. H. Bradley at Oxford and

formed his own critique of a rationalism too narrowly defined from the arguments of Kant, Hume, and, among contemporary thinkers, Henri Bergson. *All the King's Men* reveals, in addition to Ransom's influence, Warren's intimate familiarity with another figure in that tradition, the "benign and scholarly figure of William James," who, perhaps even more than Huey Long, is a pervasive presence in the novel. But the extent and sources of Warren's borrowing are less relevant here than the end toward which he borrowed, an end which is remarkably plain and consistent. As novelist and poet as well as New Critic, Warren has always sought to define the elusive sanction for art and to defend literature as a means of perceiving "truth."

The ways in which *All the King's Men* embodies these issues of "truth" and the nature of art are extremely complex. Warren's place in a venerable aesthetic tradition, however, can be clearly seen and the main terms of his position summarized. Indeed, the basic premises of it have been familiar in English literature since the Romantics. With Blake, Coleridge, and Shelley, Warren assumes that the mind is equipped with two complementary modes of perception, roughly the intellectual and the intuitive. In the modern world, however, the successful dominance of scientific technique over all other forms of discourse with the world has led to a nearly exclusive reliance upon the intellectual faculty, thus cutting man off from much of his subjective experience. But having discarded every test of experience or criterion of truth other than the laboratory, modern man has found himself in a blank, deterministic world, empty of value or significance. The scientific world view of the modern age is not "wrong," according to Warren; it represents merely too selective a discourse with the world. It is dangerous only when seen as more than a method of verifying facts and of postulating abstract laws. Scientific knowledge is *power* knowledge; it bestows control because it generalizes from experience and reduces the "world's body" to a set of useful principles. It is *pragmatically* inadequate, however, because reality—defined simply as experience—it is not abstract and not reducible to "facts." The simple test (illustrated in Burden's life) is that if man attempts to operate ethically from the premise that experience is so reducible, he immediately arrives at the dead end of alienation.

Literature, on the other hand, involves the neglected intuitive faculty and thus complements (or provides an antidote for) the limited and abstract kind of knowledge that science can bestow. It provides the "massive" and "concrete" contact with the flow of experience which science and the intellect alone cannot. It provides a kind of "knowledge" that encompasses the contradictoriness and the "irrelevance" of the subjectively felt world. Ordinary language described approximately (much like the general laws of the scientist), but in the hands of the artist, and in the crucible of a dramatic context, the ordinary imprecision of meaning is bent and twisted into fresh, original, and concrete significance; the familiar sense of a word or phrase is enriched, multiplied, charged with ambiguity, forced to coexist with and contain its contraries, made to glow with paradox. Literature, then, transcends the practical Gestalt of perception and imitates the mysterious flow of undifferentiated experience itself; it has the strange power to convey "bodily" the actual felt character of experience. The artist's power is a power to show, to reveal, rather than a power to create. Like Ahab, he can strike through the veil of the familiar and communicate uniquely and directly something of that strange, unassimilated portion of the world which remains intransigent to reason. This directness of revelation is both the chief pleasure afforded by art and its chief value.

The single story which Warren has told over and over in his fiction implies this kind of world view and aesthetic. That single story is the individual's drama of self-discovery and self-definition, a drama in which the problem of merely seeing the external world, let alone defining it, is crucial. The struggles of Warren's protagonists toward "self-knowledge" are therefore always deceptive and ambiguous; they represent (rather than arrival at final solutions) merely the process by which the mind successfully imposes pattern, value, and significance upon what Bergson called an "impenetrable flux" and William James a "pluralistic universe." That is, *self*-definition is actually the imposition of order and significance upon chaos, the creation of a "myth" sufficient to sanction and justify *action,* if not ultimately to explain the world. In Warren's depiction of this process, there is a constant analogy implied between the function of the mind in the world and the artist's ordering imagination in the work. The artist structures his material in the same way the mind discovers patterns in, or imposes them upon, experience. In the former case, the "idea" informs the structure of the work; in the latter, it shapes the values or "myth" by which one lives.

Warren's discussion of symbolism in his essay on Coleridge explicitly relates the literary device to modes of perception. The symbol, he asserts, operates as a kind of perceptual frame of reference:

> The symbol affirms the unity of the mind in the welter of
> experience: it is a device for making that welter of expe-
> rience manageable for the mind—graspable. It . . . is not a
> mere sign, a "picture language." . . . It does not stand for
> a single idea. . . . Rather a symbol implies a body of ideas
> which may be said to be fused in it.

Warren, however, is cautious about claiming to provide any ultimate
"Truth" through the medium of his art. For him, the kind of knowledge that literature imparts is "knowledge by form. No, knowledge
of form." The focus in all of his fiction is therefore on the engage-
ment of the ordering consciousness with the world, not on a pre-
sumed ultimate reality beyond the observer. The structure or form
of a Warren novel is intended as a paradigm of the *act* of experiencing, not a revelation of the object or world experienced. Insofar as
the work of art gives an image of experience being brought to order
and harmony, it is also, in Warren's words, *"myth of order* or fulfillment, an affirmation that our being may move . . . toward meaning. . . . The form [of work] gives man an image of himself, for it
gives him his mode of experiencing, a paradigm of his inner life."
Thus, the work of art *can* directly convey knowledge, knowledge at
least of the process by which man perceives. It captures the rhythm
of experience because experience is a movement toward order. What
the "reality" is that the mind organizes, Warren does not say. One
guesses that he means that the world not only seems chaotic, but
probably is, and that all experiential coherence is imposed rather than
discovered.

The general view of Warren as moralist has obscured, perhaps,
the radical skepticism implicit in his work; one may forget in the
tidiness of his resolutions of plot the extent to which his affirmations
are tentative and ironic. Warren's well-known remarks about
Conrad's world view illuminate his own, as the two are practically
identical. Conrad's skepticism, Warren claims,

> is ultimately but a "reasonable" recognition of the fact that
> man is a natural creature who can rest in no revealed values
> and can look forward to neither individual immortality
> nor racial survival. But reason, in this sense, is the denial
> of life and energy, for *against all reason man insists, as man,
> on creating and trying to live by certain values.* These values
> are, to use Conrad's word, "illusions," but *the last wisdom*

> *is for man to realize that though his values are illusions, the
> illusion is necessary, is infinitely precious, is the mark of his
> human achievement, and is, in the end, his only truth* [italics
> added].

To Warren, man is a moralizing animal, a creature who needs to
"justify himself by the 'idea,' to idealize himself and his actions into
moral significance of some order, to find sanctions." Warren suggests further that to "surrender to the incorrigible and ironical necessity of the 'idea,' that is man's fate and his only triumph."

The action in a Warren novel seems always to arise out of this
fundamental effort and conflict. As a consequence, the "world" of
any of Warren's novels is larger and more complicated than any
single vision of it articulated in the book; the inconsistencies and
contradictions in it are also presumably real and irresolvable; and the
nature of things within it eludes any final definition. Given that sense
of the limits of knowledge, Warren has insisted throughout his career
that the very act of composition must be in itself an exploration, a
"way of knowing." Such an act of creation, however (to return to
the analogy between the artist's ordering function and the difficulties
of the ordinary person in making sense of his experience), may involve the whole man and engage his entire faculties, body and soul,
head and heart, balanced and focused upon a single purpose. Thus it
may be, in a very limited sense, a temporary healing of the "terrible
divisions of the age" which Warren has often lamented. For Warren,
as for Coleridge, the creative, imaginative faculty provides the essential tie between moral man and the amoral world; "*the moral
concern and the artistic concern are aspects of the same activity, the creative
activity, and . . . this activity is expressive of the whole mind.*" A novel
such as *All the King's Men,* then, may, at the conscious level, be
"about" the tragic lack of "unity of being" in the modern world, and
at another, deeper level, it may embody the reattaining of it.

It is appropriate, then, that the story of Jack Burden's initiation
be constructed in the form of a quest, or rather a series of quests, on
which he—a self-proclaimed "student of history"—embarks. Burden's attitudes are representatively modern; his claim to be an objective seeker of "facts" is the best clue to his alienation. He embodies
the "terrible divisions" of modern times in his habitual insistence
upon a rational, overly intellectual response to experience. His characteristic stance is moral neutrality; he is wholly devoid of any *con-*

scious moral standards or allegiances. Paradoxically, Burden is an "innocent," if only in the root meaning of the word. He knows practically nothing of the world or of himself; or rather, what he knows amounts to a few cynical generalizations, a few isolated facts. He can see neither himself nor his world "whole," and he can sense no relationship between himself and his "facts." Like the masses who support Stark, he has little conception of his personal worth and can see no discernible reason why he ought to have. His several quests, all of which are attempts to understand some portion of the world, overlap significantly and in such a way that Jack eventually sees that the solution of a single riddle might be the answer to them all. His effort to resolve the enigma which is Willie Stark is simultaneously an effort to resolve the enigma which is Jack Burden. Roughly the same is true of the story of Cass Mastern, the subject of his unfinished Ph.D. dissertation. In both these efforts and in the quest that provides the mainspring of the plot, the issue at hand appears to Jack to be a mere question of *fact*. He is not conscious of any metaphysical implications in Stark's order to dig into the past of Jack's old friend and mentor, Judge Irwin. The purpose of Jack's search, which he mockingly calls the "Case of the Upright Judge," is simply to find something that can be used to destroy the judge politically.

For a political hatchet man in the Stark administration, however, Jack takes a strangely bemused and detached attitude toward his work, viewing the circus side show of greed and ambition from what he takes to be a lofty and nonpartisan philosophical perspective. He carefully divorces himself from both the ethical questions and the consequences of his "research": things, after all, are the way they are through no fault of his: "I was a very thorough and well-trained research student. And truth was what I sought, without fear or favor. And let the chips fly." Nothing that he finds or does, or so Jack likes to believe, has any connection with him, a mere "student" of history. This pose of objectivity is both a mask for his larger alienation and an attempt to make himself less vulnerable. Living in a world which he feels is empty of value, Jack is consumed with self-contempt, regards himself practically as a nonentity, and is profoundly pessimistic about what can be accomplished in life. He has no interest in the future because he unconsciously assumes that there is nothing worth doing, nothing, at any rate, that he could do. His remark to Anne Stanton that he lacks "ambition" is an understatement. He not only lacks ambition, but all "essential confidence" in himself and in the world. It is one of the ironies of the novel that Jack, who believes that no action of his could be of any consequence, sets in motion a train of events which brings tragedy to everyone close to him.

Jack's state of mind early in the novel closely resembles that moral numbness of several early Hemingway characters: the Nick Adams of "Big Two-Hearted River" or Krebs of "Soldier's Home." Jack has the precarious self-control of the psychically wounded. His cynicism seems, like the stoicism of a Hemingway character, partly a defensive strategy aimed at keeping himself functioning. Even the specious "Idealism" in which he pretends to believe is a device to distance himself from what is going on around him: "I had got hold of the principle out of a book when I was in college, and I had hung on to it for grim death. I owed my success in life to that principle. It had put me where I was. What you don't know don't hurt you, for it ain't real." At the same time, his attitudes reflect the consequences of a belief in the mythology of "scientism." In fact, the two greatest intellectual obstacles to his discovery of coherence in his life, Willie Stark's amoral pragmatism and his own crude pseudoscientific determinism (which Jack sardonically labels "The Great Twitch"), also embody the assumptions of scientism. Those assumptions, which Warren has called the "nightmare" of the age, are the nightmare from which Jack Burden struggles so painfully to awake. One lesson in that awakening is the discovery of his own vulnerability, his own pain, in spite of his intellectual posing. The role of observer in the safety of the laboratory, he discovers, is not available to him in the confusion of the world. The "student of history" is not exempt from the "facts" that he exhumes, for the inert "facts" have a way of becoming "truth" and impinging upon his own life. The "perfect research job" which Jack performs on Judge Irwin's past is thus "marred in its technical perfection by only one thing: it meant something." What it means is that Jack is responsible for the suicide of his own father, that by a "fatal appropriateness" he has handed over the woman he loves to another man and his two best friends over to death.

While it is immediately apparent that the Irwin assignment is an important test of Jack's character, its full significance (like the "true identity" of Judge Irwin) is carefully withheld. The assignment is the first real conflict of loyalties Jack encounters in his job with Stark, and it forces his previous values and allegiances (most of which he denies having) into sharp definition. But that is only a part of the significance of the assignment; its full impact can be understood only in terms of the near nihilism of Jack's early outlook. Warren allows the reader to grasp only gradually the full significance of what Jack has at stake in the "Case of the Upright Judge" by allowing a series of glimpses of the interior landscape of his protagonist's mind. Warren is able to dramatize with an unusual intimacy and directness how Jack and several other characters perceive the world by depicting a few of their symbolic "pictures" of it. In those pictures, Warren implies, lie the values by which they unconsciously live. William James described a similar method of psychological orientation in *The Varieties of Religious Experience*. Such pictures of the world

> form the background for all our facts, the fountainhead of all the possibilities we conceive of. They give its "nature," as we call it, to every special thing. Everything we know is "what" it is by sharing in the nature of one of these abstractions. We can never look directly at them, for they are bodiless and featureless and footless, but we grasp all other things by their means, and in handling the real world we should be stricken with helplessness in just so far forth as we might lose these mental objects, these . . . heads of classification and conception.

Through this device Warren extends the analogy between the technique of the artist and the imagination in general: the artist's symbols correspond to these emotion and value-charged pictures of the world. Both are devices for rendering the "welter of experience manageable for the mind."

Jack's vision of Anne Stanton as a young girl, when Jack was only seventeen and not yet in love with her, is one of a number of such pictures which form his attitudes toward the world. What he sees is merely a slender, dark-haired girl floating effortlessly in the sea, with her face turned serenely upward toward the ominously darkened storm clouds as a single white gull passes overhead. Yet the memory of that moment sticks in Jack's mind; it marks an internal rather than an external event, a sudden quantum jump in his awareness:

> I suppose that that day I first saw Anne and Adam as separate, individual people, whose ways of acting were

special, mysterious, and important. And perhaps, too, that day I first saw myself as a person. But that is not what I am talking about. What happened was this: I got an image in my head that never got out. We see a great many things and can remember a great many things, but that is different. We get very few of the true images in our heads of the kind I am talking about, the kind which become more and more vivid for us as if the passage of years did not obscure their reality but, year by year, drew off another veil to expose a meaning which we had only dimly surmised at first. Very probably the last veil will not be removed, for there are not enough years, but the brightness of the image increases and our conviction increases that the brightness is meaning, or the legend of meaning, and without the image our lives would be nothing except an old piece of film rolled on a spool and thrown into a desk drawer among the unanswered letters.

These images, which are mute until Jack has acquired sufficient experience to interpret them, are emblems of his "truth," the shape of the things by which he lives.

It might be said that in his bleaker moments Jack aspires to the condition of the spool of film, to that total passiveness and unconsciousness of the recording instrument on which experience is merely imprinted objectively, without pattern or meaning. But Jack discovers he cannot live as an unconscious, naturalistic mechanism. Even in his last and most profound self-deception, his period of belief in a simple determinism which he calls the Great Twitch, Jack cannot silence the question that rises in him: "if the twitch was all, what was it that could know that the twitch was all?" And in his long period of cynicism during which he is convinced he believes in nothing, he finds that he had been living "unwittingly" by the values he had unconsciously associated with his picture of Anne Stanton.

The sources of Jack's general cynicism and apathy are partly discernible in his mental images of his parents. In fact, at one level, his quest is a search for a father. The image of Ellis Burden which Jack remembers from childhood is of a "thick-set, strong man, not tall, with a shock of tangled black hair on his head and steel-rimmed glasses on his nose and a habit of buttoning up his vest wrong, and a big gold watch chain, which I liked to pull at." That kindly and ineffectual man, whom Jack later dubbed the Scholarly Attorney, had walked out of his home and buried himself in the slums where he lived in fanatical seclusion, handing out tracts and caring for "unfortunates." The disheveled, myopic ruin of a man whom Jack visits in the slums seems to him a terrible fulfillment of qualities latent in the earlier picture. What Jack thinks he sees in Ellis Burden is an abject failure, a man who, in the most fundamental ways, has not measured up. It is Jack who makes the coarse and speculative judgment of Ellis which he attributes to casual observers of his family's break up: "He was a queer 'un. Damn if he wasn't queer, going off and leaving a real looker like that woman out of Arkansas. Maybe he couldn't give her what she craved." As Jack tells Anne, "I know the truth. I know what my mother is like. . . . And I know my father was a fool to let her get him down."

Jack's image of his mother similarly contributes to his nearly paralyzing self-doubts. Jack sees her as a beautiful but shallow, hollow-cheeked temptress who changes the men in her life as casually as she changes the graceful antique furniture in the big house at Burden's Landing. She seems to him incapable of genuine affection. He is both drawn and repelled by the attention she bestows upon him and the other men in her life. But as Jack is painfully aware, the recurrent scene of his homecoming resembles the welcome of a woman for her lover as much as the greeting of a mother for her son. She is a woman of few words, and her gestures, though eloquent, seem to Jack calculated rather than expressive: "she didn't really care a thing about me. . . . I was just another man whom she wanted to have around because she was the kind of woman who had to have men around and had to make them dance to her tune."

These two bleak pictures of his parents provide the basic lenses through which Jack views the world. And inevitably, as Jack's indictment of his parents colors his view of the rest of the world, it taints his view of himself as well, hence Jack's lack of confidence in himself during his early relationship with Anne, and his moral shock in graduate school when he reads the diary of Cass Mastern and sees consequences proceeding out of a single act with the inevitability of limbs from a tree and leaves from a bough. Jack cannot comprehend, or cannot face, a view of the world in which actions have consequences, for to him the world "was simply an accumulation of items, odds and ends of things like the broken and misused and dust-shrouded things gathered in a garret. Or it was a flux of things before his eyes (or behind his eyes) and one thing had nothing to do, in the end, with anything else." In such a world, naturally enough, Jack can find no motive for acting and no conviction that his acts have any meaning.

There are, to be sure, contradictory or anomalous elements in Jack's pictures of the world, and some of them alleviate this pervasive gloom. Chief among those anomalies is his picture of Anne Stanton, vulnerable and innocent under an ominous sky. What she represents to him is perhaps all the more precious by virtue of its being unconnected to anything else in the world. One other exception is his picture of an erect, hawk-faced man who had been the best friend of Ellis Burden and the teacher and friend of Jack himself during his childhood. That figure, of course, is Judge Montague Irwin, the man into whose past Jack is ordered to dig.

Given Jack's general outlook, pieced together from these several images of the world, the momentousness of Stark's order to investigate Irwin's past can easily be seen. Jack's picture of the judge is another of those things by which he unconsciously lives, one of the few ideals remaining to him, perhaps the only one outside of Anne Stanton. As a consequence, Jack has an immense stake in that quest, for it involves not just the guilt or innocence of one man, but the general nature of things. To Jack, Irwin represents an ultimate of a kind, and on the revelation of what his life has been hangs one of Jack's last hopes. "But suppose," Jack objects to Stark, "there isn't anything to find?" "There is always something," the Governor replies.

Much of the action of *All the King's Men* is thus a recounting of the process by which Jack Burden revises his understanding of his various pictures of the world. The experiences he endures and the knowledge he acquires result in the lifting of veil after veil from the bright images in his mind until he is, in a sense, reborn. The symbolic import of Jack's vision of Anne floating in the bay becomes clear to him, for instance, only years after the event, as he is about to consummate their love affair. For Jack, however, the high point of their early relationship had come earlier, in an embrace under water after Anne had taken the highest and most reckless dive of her life. The ecstacy of their kiss in that weightless and womb-like privacy underwater reminds Jack of his first discovery that he was in love. The state of suspension, of total isolation from the ordinary world at the moment of their kiss, is an emblem of Jack's habitual state of mind. There, for a moment, they exist like the lovers on Keats's Grecian Urn. Nothing is connected to anything else; they are outside of time. On the other hand, with Anne in his bedroom, the consummation toward which their relationship had been moving all summer vaguely alarms Jack. That moment, simply by its nature as a consummation, is decidedly not out of time. It is the irrevocable end of something and the beginning of something else. As Jack is about to take Anne, her passively reclining figure reminds him of an earlier scene:

> At the instant when she closed her eyes, as I stared at her, my mind took one of the crazy leaps and I saw her floating in the water, that day of the picnic three years before, with her eyes closed and the violent sky above and the white gull flashing high over, and that face and this face and that scene and this scene seemed to fuse, like superimposed photographs, each keeping its identity but without denying the other. And at that instant, as I stood there . . . I looked at her on the iron bed . . . and knew that everything was wrong, completely wrong, how I didn't know, didn't try to know, and that this was somehow not what the summer had been driving toward. That I wasn't going to do it.

This moment reveals to Jack that he had been living unconsciously by the values he had attached to that earlier picture of Anne. What that picture represents is a fragile innocence and beauty which is, he thinks, exempt from the murk and welter of the rest of the world. He finds he cannot take Anne sexually without violating his image of her. As he understands years later, he could not willingly "plunge her into the full, dark stream of the world," lacking as he did an "essential confidence" in himself.

Jack's hesitation is a refusal to "know" Anne, both literally and figuratively, for the girl lying on the bed waiting for him is not an idealized figure on a Grecian Urn but a live woman who is exempt from nothing whether he plunges her into the dark stream of time or not. She is already in it, and by choosing the image he loses the reality and, later on, the image as well. Jack sees all this, to his horror, some fifteen years later, after he discovers the "truth" about Judge Irwin's past and after that truth had made Anne the mistress of Willie Stark:

> I saw the little creases in the flesh of her neck, just the
> tiniest little creases, the little mark left day after day by that
> absolutely infinitesimal gossamer cord of thuggee which
> time throws around the prettiest neck every day to garrote
> it. The cord is so gossamer that it breaks every day, but the
> marks get there finally, and finally one day the gossamer
> cord doesn't break and is enough.

Jack is struck by that perception as if by a blow. He realizes, in
another flash of revelation, that the "truth" he had deduced from his
picture of Anne Stanton and which he had been living by had been
a illusion.

That knowledge comes as a belated and partial insight after
years of willful ignorance and self-deception. Jack had long occupied
himself with various conscious and half-conscious strategies of denial
and resistance to that knowledge: his "Idealism," his crude, mechan-
ically gratifying hedonism in his marriage to Lois, and the death-like
oblivion of his periodic "Great Sleeps." But his chief distraction is to
allow himself to be caught up in the momentum of Willie Stark's
career and to accept, without much reflection, the Governor's working philosophy. Being aimless himself, he consents to being aimed
by Stark. It is the refutation of Stark's philosophy, *his* picture of the
world, by the events leading up to and including the assassination,
which forces Jack's complete reevaluation of himself and eventually
leads him out of the nihilism of his early adult life.

In Jack's experience, Willie's assumptions are the only ones that
actually work. The confusion of other men seems, in fact, that element in which Stark moves—confidently, purposefully, and successfully. Willie's homespun philosophy is a grab bag of half-truths as
inconsistent as they are practically effective. From his Presbyterian
upbringing Stark had appropriated a convenient belief in the universal depravity of man: "There is always something"; "You don't ever
have to frame anybody, because the truth is always sufficient." Stark
also professes a belief in a simple determinism, which he labels the
"nature of things." "There ain't any explanation," he asserts to Jack.
"Not of anything. All you can do is point to the nature of things."
Stark's philosophy, because it posits an amoral universe in which
nothing can be done about fundamentals and in which what is given
might as well be used, frees him from the necessity of scrutinizing his
own behavior too carefully and thus also frees him, though it is a

dangerous and illusory freedom, to act as he chooses. Ironically, Stark's primitive determinism (like the Calvinism of the Puritans) provides him with a rationale for the aggressive exercise of his will. Another major component of Stark's philosophy is his pragmatism, a habit of mind which recognizes no moral absolutes and which focuses upon ends, on results, rather than on means. Stark's pragmatism has little logical connection with the other tenets of his philosophy, but his whole world view does have a psychological consistency. Again, what he believes affords him a license to *act,* however poorly it explains the world.

Stark takes a Hobbesian view of human society; any historical situation consists, he thinks, of "a lot of folks wrassling around." If such conflict is universal, it becomes, in a sense, morally neutral, a simple given; and thus, as Stark insists, everything depends upon what one does with that given. In Stark's view, moral categories are arbitrary and impermanent; they are chiefly nuisances that hinder effective action. Right, he says, "is a lid you put on something and some of the things under the lid look just like some of the things not under the lid." Moral notions are never adequate for getting the necessary human business done. And that business *must* be done. Frustrated, it becomes, like the steam in a bottle, capable of producing an explosion. "But you put it in the right place and let it out in a certain way and it will run a freight engine." As he tells people who object to his tactics: you can't make bricks without straw, and most of the "straw" has to come from the cowpen. Goodness, he explains, has to be made out of badness "because there isn't anything else to make it out of." How this miraculous transformation occurs is simple enough in Stark's view: "You just make it up as you go along."

Jack is fascinated by the Boss's complete moral relativism. The Governor admits freely that he has crooks in his administration, and that they represent some "energy loss" in the form of state funds leaked into their pockets. But he insists that something is delivered in return:

> "Sure, there's some graft, but there's just enough to make the wheels turn without squeaking. And remember this. There never was a machine rigged up by man didn't represent some loss of energy. How much energy do you get out of a lump of coal when you run a steam dynamo or

a locomotive compared to what there actually is in that
lump of coal?"

Stark's view of things, however, rests as much as Jack's upon a
process of selective blindness. The contradictions between Stark's
belief in determinism and universal human depravity and the way he
acts about his hospital project, for instance, imply an unspoken and
perhaps unconscious premise. Man is a part of predetermined nature;
Stark, however, is exempt. All men are evil; he, Willie Stark, can
make good out of evil. These prerogatives which Stark unconsciously
claims for himself extend themselves as he grows used to the exercise
of power. The irremediable injury which his son Tom receives is
therefore a decisive shock to his world view. He had regarded the
boy virtually as an *alter ego,* and Tom's injury demonstrated that
Stark cannot control even what he had conceived to be an extension
of himself. When Stark tries to reform and "make everything right,"
he discovers there are consequences arising from his previous actions
that continue regardless of his change of heart or his will to atone.
The hospital project, the one accomplishment he had wanted to keep
"pure," becomes indirectly the instrument of his own doom. And,
ironically, his attempts to atone for his sins lead to his assassination.
Ultimately, Stark himself demonstrates that he does not believe in
the moral relativism that he expounds and he repudiates it. On his
deathbed Stark avows that "it might have all been different," thus
acknowledging his own freedom to have acted otherwise. "You got
to believe that," he says to Jack.

The collapse of the only workable values Jack has seen provides
yet another of the shocks that bring Jack to a new understanding of
the world. The nature of Jack's new picture of reality is difficult to
describe, and its precise nature is perhaps less significant than the
process by which Jack attains it. That new picture is influenced by a
large and complex body of experience whose import Jack simply
cannot escape or deny. He comes to realize that by digging up the
presumably "dead" past he has set in motion a chain of unforeseen
events which have had tragic consequences for everyone he loved.
His discovery, belated and expensive as it is, demonstrates to him
the interconnections among all things in a *moral* rather than a
mechanistic order. Or rather, he discovers that the order in his
experience is simultaneously mechanistic and moral, and that to
"handle" it as exclusively one or the other is fatal. Jack learns, just as

Cass Mastern had, that these connections among events are totally unpredictable:

> He learned that the world is all of one piece. He learned that the world is like an enormous spider web and if you touch it, however lightly, at any point, the vibration ripples to the remotest perimeter and the drowsy spider feels the tingle and is drowsy no more but springs out to fling the gossamer coils about you who have touched the web. . . . It does not matter whether or not you meant to brush the web of things.

His sense of the doubleness of experience is summed up very well in Hugh Miller's epigram: "History is blind, but man is not." Jack finally has to accept (whether he understands it or not) his position both in and outside of the chain of cause and effect, where (in Whitman's words) he remains, "watching and wondering at it."

William James's concept of a "pluralistic universe" is useful here in clarifying Jack's new attitudes. James assumed that the world could *only* be accounted for in terms of such unresolved contradictions:

> What, in the end, are all our verifications but experiences that agree with more or less isolated systems of ideas . . . that our minds have framed? But why in the name of common sense need we assume that only one such system of ideas can be true? The obvious outcome of our total experience is that the world can be handled according to many systems of ideas.

If the same data yield distinct or contradictory generalizations, then both may be true. In the matter of his father's death, for instance, Jack sees that he is both responsible for Irwin's suicide and hence a murderer and simultaneously a "blameless instrument" of justice. He sees also that his two friends, Adam Stanton and Willie Stark, were "doomed" to destroy each other, though each lived in the "agony of will."

Thus, as a result of his experience, and not because of further speculation, Jack comes to reject the Great Twitch as a partial view which contains nothing he can live by: "He did not believe in it because he had seen too many people live and die. . . . And the ways of their living had nothing to do with the Great Twitch." Similarly, in what had previously seemed only a clutter of pain and meaningless struggle in the lives around Jack, he begins to perceive pattern and meaning: in the lives of his friends there had been similar blunderings toward understanding, and he learns that his own confusion and error had been shared by others, had represented, in fact, their common experience as human beings. Thus, Jack's "redemption" is not a matter of specific conclusions about the world, but a deeper, more visceral change. His rebirth is not precipitated by an intellectual discovery but by a sudden outpouring of love. Like Coleridge's Ancient Mariner, Jack suddenly and involuntarily "blesses" the life around him and sees beauty where he had previously seen deformity. The moment of transcendence is appropriately the sudden perception of the bond between himself and his mother and, symbolically, the bond between himself and his past. The change in Jack is a new receptivity to experience and a less exclusive reliance upon his intellect to interpret and judge it: "I was willing to let those speculations rest," he says. "I dismissed the question, and dismissed the answer I had tried to give it, and simply held . . . [my mother's] lax hand between my own." Jack ceases his restless dissections of things, accepting a viewpoint close to William James's notion of a "radical" empiricism: a belief that all aspects of experience, not just those elements amenable to rational analysis, must be taken into account as "real."

It would be inaccurate, however, to conclude that Jack's world view at the end represents some final version of the truth. Several other characters, including Stark, Sugar-Boy, Anne Stanton, Sadie Burke, and Lucy Stark, also alter their views of reality, and those views do not concur at all points with Jack's. Lucy Stark, for instance, finds solace in her belief that the baby she has adopted is Tom's and in her conviction that Willie had been truly great. These are beliefs which must seem to Jack, in spite of all his sympathy, blind and wish-fulfilling. But they are practically adequate for Lucy; her beliefs provide her the terms on which she can live, and she goes on, as Jack does. It would seem, then, that Warren embraces a relativism even more radical and arbitrary than Stark's, and implies that the purely subjective vision is all that is possible. What is believed to be true *is* true, and it is true *because* it is believed. Whatever has "real" effects is itself real.

That impression is not left unqualified, however. While Jack can see the necessity of Lucy's beliefs, he is not moved to abandon himself to subjectivism. It is as if Jack has learned that there is a point where one's conceptions of the world, one's "myths," as it were, leave off, and the world (*whatever* it is) begins. On the one hand, Jack realizes that his false *sense* of himself has had fatal consequences to others, and he recognizes the "peculiar appropriateness" in the co-incidence that what *he* tells Anne makes her Stark's mistress. But on the other hand, other events in his life have had their "real" effects regardless of any belief of his about them. There is thus a literal duplicity, a doubleness, in every aspect of Jack's experience. He confronts a world that arrays itself in an endless, impenetrable "di-alectical configuration" of contradictions. It both eludes and exceeds any sense he can make of it.

Even at the end, Jack finds such contradictions unresolvable. The practical problems they pose are suggested in his encounter with a reporter at Stark's funeral who condemns him for his collaboration with the Stark regime: "The trouble is," Jack concludes, "they are half right and half wrong, and in the end that is what paralyzes you." To avoid being paralyzed, Jack must reject, illogically, belief both in moral absolutes *and* in complete relativity. That precarious equilib-rium is imaged in Jack's discovery of the "true lie." While he cannot concur with the reasons for Lucy's faith in Stark's greatness, for instance, he agrees with her conclusion. And while he lies to his mother about what happened between Judge Irwin and himself just prior to Irwin's suicide, what Jack tells her is the "truth." Irwin had not been in any "jam" when he died. Something of the man re-mained untouched and untainted by the crimes he had committed. There is even a sense in which the conversation with Jack *was* Irwin's salvation and in which the Judge "redeemed" himself by putting a bullet through his heart.

Rather than finally learning to explain the world rationally, Jack learns merely to live in it, and he can do that only when he accepts his experience in its original fullness and particularity and "impu-rity." By abandoning his attempts to define his experience, Jack is able to heal, partially at least, those divisions in man with which the Agrarians had been concerned. His redemption consists not in any lasting certitude or perfect happiness, but in the attainment of a full, unified response to experience: he can at last see the world steadily, and see it whole. That is to say, he has knowledge of the "world's body" but no blueprint of it.

From Politics to Psychology: Warren's *All the King's Men*

Richard H. King

More than any other southern novelist, Robert Penn Warren has been concerned in his writing with exploring ethical and philosophical issues. Indeed, Warren's weakness as a novelist has been a proclivity to preach at his characters and at his readers, and to philosophize. As Roger Sale has asserted, the conflict between Warren's talent for story-telling and his interest in striking off profundities compromises the quality of his fiction. This judgment is not confined to outsiders and non-Southerners. No less than John Crowe Ransom voiced similar misgivings when he wrote to Allen Tate about *World Enough and Time* that Warren's worldview led "him to philosophize sententiously about Truth, Innocence, Justice and what not."

Such a comment is particularly ironic in light of the Agrarian animus against "abstraction" and Warren's own insistence that Southerners display a deep-seated suspicion of "abstraction." By abstraction the Agrarians referred, first, to the scientific-technological vision of reality and, second, to the efforts of political liberals and radicals to run roughshod over human nature in the name of social change. Warren preserved the spirit of this double-barreled critique of abstraction, but by the post–World War II years his attacks on the spirit of abstraction fit easily into the dominant cultural mood, which stressed the non-ideological and non-doctrinaire nature of the American experience as an antidote to the dogmatic rigidity and ideological horrors of Stalinist Russia. Closer to home, for Warren (and

From *A Southern Renaissance: The Cultural Awakening of the American South 1930–1955.*
© 1980 by Oxford University Press.

C. Vann Woodward) the South was to play America to the North's "Russia." The South exemplified a sort of historical reality principle that might keep the nation on an even keel. This was a southern version of the end-of-ideology thesis that appealed so to many chastened liberals in those years.

The philosophical underpinnings of Warren's writing combine existentialist themes and vaguely pyschoanalytic motifs. Prominent among them are the search for identity and self, the problem of human freedom, the complex relationship of past and present, with the saving power of the *deus ex machina* "love" thrown in for good measure. For Warren, man's chief end is knowledge of the human condition; and it is this knowledge, as expressed in poetry and fiction, that reconciles man to his fate and returns him to a union and communion with nature and others. Thus, there is in Warren's view a movement from alienation from self and others through trials and tests to a reconciliation with self and others, a self-acceptance and hence acceptance of others. This pattern of secular salvation, a moral therapeutic and modern mythological heroic, provides the conceptual underpinning for all of Warren's fiction. But because Warren's stories must conform to this procrustean conceptual schema, the moments of insights and reconciliations at the climax of his novels often seem willed and unearned in the context of the story.

Warren was one of the pioneering practitioners of the New Criticism. More important, Warren championed Faulkner as early as 1930; and his lengthy review-essay of Malcolm Cowley's *The Portable Faulkner* in 1946 helped mightily to rehabilitate Faulkner's reputation. Warren's essay was marked by the desire to claim for Faulkner more than "regional" significance. The Mississippian was clearly, for Warren, a writer of universal import. "The legend," he wrote, "is not merely a legend of the South, but is also a legend of our general plight and problem. The modern world is in moral confusion." More important, there was in Faulkner's work a "constant ethical center . . . to be found in the glorification of the human effort and human endurance."

Several things need to be said about Warren's reading of Faulkner. First, it says as much about Warren's intentions as a novelist as it does about Faulkner's. Second, Warren's "ethical" reading of Faulkner increasingly carried the day in the critical rediscovery and rehabilitation of Faulkner in the 1950s. In his essay Warren took several swipes at left-wing critics, particularly Maxwell Geismar, who considered Faulkner a reactionary and proto-fascist. In that sense Warren's defense-*cum*-appreciation was a valuable corrective. But, it went too far in the other direction and read back into Faulkner's great work of the 1930s what was barely emerging in *Go Down, Moses.* Warren's ethical and universalizing reading comported all too well with what was weakest in Faulkner, something the publication of *A Fable* revealed.

Faulkner's verdict on Warren's *All the King's Men* revealed a proper suspicion of striving for the large effect. After reading the galleys of Warren's soon-to-published novel, Faulkner responded (to Warren's publisher) that the "Cass Mastern story is a beautiful and moving piece. That was his novel. The rest of it I would throw away." (In the novel Jack Burden was once a graduate student working on a doctoral dissertation in history. For his project he must read through the letters of Cass Mastern, a distant relative of his father's. The story he pieces together from the surviving documents concerns Mastern's affair with a close friend's wife, the friend's suicide, and Mastern's subsequent effort to expiate his "sin" by freeing his slaves and taking responsibility for what he has done. Mastern dies in the Civil War in 1864.) Though Faulkner's judgment is too harsh, it still displays a certain cogency. In telling the Mastern story, Warren allows the implications to emerge on their own rather than telling the reader how to interpret it. (The same judgment applies to *A Fable;* the embedded story of the jockey is a small masterpiece, vintage Faulkner, but the rest could have been discarded.) Thus in his desire to be a worthy successor of Faulkner, Warren misread Faulkner to bring him into line with his own proclivities and constitute him as a precursor of Warren's own concerns.

Though one of the original Fugitive-Agrarians, Warren was the youngest and least tied to Agrarianism as a creed. From early on he ranged more widely than most of his Vanderbilt colleagues and has by now important work to his credit in almost every literary genre. Coming as he does from south-central Kentucky, Warren had ties, like Wolfe's and Agee's, much more with the up-country South and the hard-scrabble world of the small farmer than with the black-belt or the aristocratic legacy of the old South. There is little nostalgia in Warren's work for the culture of the family romance, at least in any specific historical sense. And though the father-son theme is central in his work, it lacks the historical-cultural resonance found in Faulkner or Tate.

Warren's *All the King's Men* belongs with V. O. Key's *Southern Politics* and C. Vann Woodward's several works as major efforts to explore the cultural implications of the "revolt of the rednecks" against the conservative Democratic hegemony, the repository, albeit a highly compromised one, of the tradition of the family romance in southern politics. Admittedly, though not exclusively, modeled on the career of Huey Long, the novel was organized around a fictional situation remarkably similar to the one so vividly (and bitterly) described by Will Percy in *Lanterns on the Levee.* In both cases the old order of commercial, industrial, and agricultural interests, overlain with a patina of aristocratic prestige, faced a challenge from the poor farmers and the hill people.

But unlike the Delta aristocrat, Warren's sympathies did not lie exclusively with the forces of order and stability. Though one can scarcely identify the ideological sympathies of the novelist (particularly a good one) with any certainty, Warren's fictional treatment of Willie Stark is by no means hostile. In fact, some early reviewers of *All the King's Men* claimed that Warren had whitewashed Stark (whom they saw as a thinly disguised Huey Long) and thus glorified a home-grown form of fascism. Whatever the faults of *All the King's Men,* its superiority to the rest of Warren's fiction lies in the genuine though not uncritical sympathy which Warren shows for all his main characters. In other of his novels, especially *Night Riders* and *World Enough and Time,* Warren seems deliberately to load the dice against his protagonist, who is usually a blind idealist, possessed by an *idée fixe,* and over his head in the sea of history. As a result the central figures lack a certain life of their own and fail to compel our interest.

Though Jack Burden eventually rejects Stark's strong-arm tactics and the atmosphere of intimidation which he encouraged, even thrived on, Jack does attempt to understand the personal and political forces that made Willie run. Willie wants to do "good"; and indeed he had. But besides doing good, Stark wants power for its own sake, not merely to defeat opponents but to humiliate them. This is perhaps his main flaw. But the flaw is made comprehensible in the political context of the book: it is "earned." Nor does Warren make Stark a figure of energy and charisma without intelligence. Stark knows what he wants to do with his power and knows how to go about doing it. His sheer intelligence is more than a match for that of any of his enemies or his friends.

Warren's treatment of Stark also anticipates V. O. Key's contention that southern politics has more often than not been a contest of personalities rather than of principles. Stark's political movement is based on an impulse rather than any very coherent ideology. This is not to deny that Stark has principles and a program of sorts. But the Stark machine is built on no coherent ideology shared by his lieutenants and his followers. It rather depends on Willie's personal qualities and his ability to tap the emotions of his supporters. That Jack Burden, whose sympathies initially lie with Willie, could so easily abandon his cause indicates the ideological vacuum and the lack of staying power of southern middle-class liberalism. Neither Willie nor Tom Watson was an educator as well as a leader. But unlike Watson, Stark makes no appeal to racism and nativism. Such impulses are not central to Stark's (or Long's) appeal; and he "luckily" dies before he might have been tempted to use them. *All the King's Men* was thus the first attempt by a southern novelist to treat a Populist-type movement and its leader sympathetically and even-handedly.

The question must also be raised to the extent to which *All the King's Men* is importantly a southern novel as opposed to being a novel set in the South. The brilliant opening pages of the work show Warren's ability to render a mood and ambience in full and startling concreteness. The atmosphere is *echt*-southern; of that there can be no doubt. But, unlike the fiction of Tate, Faulkner, or Lillian Smith and like the writings of Agee and Wolfe, the South as an historical-cultural entity is not thematized in any clear-cut way. To be sure Judge Irwin is, for example, a representative of the old planter class, a figure much like Leroy Percy in his combination of Old South manner and New South connections; but his significance in the novel does not depend upon these characteristics. Neither his life nor death raises questions of regional import; the decline of the old way of life and the triumph of the new commercialism are only mutedly introduced as themes. Richard Gray has asserted that *All the King's Men* is typically southern in its concern with the way past and present are inextricably linked. That is certainly a central theme of the novel, but that is precisely the problem: its generality. Surely all sorts of works in modernist literature are organized around this theme without thereby making them uniquely southern.

Thus in *All the King's Men,* and in most of Warren's fiction, the South serves as a setting rather than a theme itself. More important, Warren's dominant concern in *All the King's Men* is less an evaluation of the collective southern past than, first, an exploration of the problem of power and political insurgency and, second, of self-definition and identity. This latter concern is closely related to Warren's standing concern with the relation of past and present. But in *All the King's Men,* unlike *Absalom, Absalom!* or "The Bear," this crucial relation is problematic for an individual, Jack Burden. It is *his* problem and not that of the region as a whole. The wider symbolic resonance is simply not there.

The central concerns of *All the King's Men* are closely linked to a vexing formal problem in the novel: the status of Jack Burden's narrative and the credibility of what he says. Early critics of *All the King's Men* too easily confused Burden's first-person, retrospective narrative with Warren's own point of view; and defenders of the novel properly warned against such an identification. Yet, as Sale observes, Warren seems to want it both ways. Clearly, for instance, Jack abandons his "great twitch" view of human action and responsibility for a position that makes the individual ultimately responsible for his own actions and the implications of those actions—the "spider web" view. He comes to see this as the meaning of the Cass Mastern story. His discovery of the story as a graduate student in history and his working through the letters and extant documents parallels his later, less disinterested attempt to dig up dirt on Judge Irwin. What Jack learns from the Cass Mastern episode eventually enables him to transcend his past and live in the future. Only when he absorbs what the Cass Mastern story has to tell him can he complete the job of writing up the story. Finally, Jack's use of the Cass Mastern story as a moral touchstone repeats Ike's and Quentin's obsession with the pasts of their families. But, again, the regional implication is absent in Jack's case.

There is, one cannot help feeling, a certain anticlimactic quality about Jack's birth into moral responsibility at the end of the novel. Jack takes no action as a concrete token of his responsibility, at least none that matches Cass's freeing of his slaves. Intellectually and emotionally he acknowledges his responsibility in the complex of events that leads to the deaths of Irwin, Stark, and Adam Stanton; and through his conversation with his mother he comes to accept his own past. But this recognition and acknowledgment lead to no wider responsibility nor do they demand anything of him. Unlike Ike McCaslin, who abjures his land and loses his wife, Jack, like Job, gets everything back: he gains a wife and an inheritance of money and property.

For most of the novel Jack is a cynical, know-it-all, pseudo-tough-guy who sounds more like a character from Hemingway than Faulkner and whose flip posturing is meant to signal his alienation from others and himself. Because he cannot solve the riddle of his own past and discover the significance of the Cass Mastern story, he lacks a future. Still, as narrator, Jack gives us clues all the way through that this is his preenlightened incarnation. It is Jack himself who dissects his own values and action. This in itself helps Warren avoid some of the faults of his later novels.

Jack's birth into insight comes when he learns who his real father is. At the beginning Jack plays a pliable but aware son to Stark's strong father. As with the Quentin-Sutpen connection in *Absalom, Absalom!* consciousness and action, passivity and activity are divided between two characters, a device that mirrors the central spiritual problem of the novel: the alienation of self from self, of past from present, of father from son. Jack's distasteful political task of blackmailing Judge Irwin leads to the suicide of the Judge. Jack then learns from his mother that the Judge, not the weak Ellis Burden, is his father. The price of such knowledge is always high, though always necessary as well, in Warren's work. As Jack says: "Well, I had swapped the good, weak father for the evil, strong one . . . I had dug up the truth and the truth always kills the father . . . and you are left alone with yourself and the truth, and can never ask Dad, who didn't know anyway and who is deader than a mackerel." Within the action of the novel, the son slays the father and gains insight; the wiser narrator Jack kills off his earlier incarnations; and the author rewards Jack as God rewards Job.

The implications of this passage are crucial to understanding the novel, but their effect is weakened by a certain confusion and lapse in tone. To find the truth about one's own past, Warren says, often involves suffering and even violence. The father possesses or stands for what one must know, and the knowledge wrested from him leads to freedom and responsibility. Only by acquiring this knowledge of his family's past and learning the true feelings of his mother can Jack acquire a future, which is to say a self that can act freely. Jack's (pseudo-) ancestor, Cass Mastern, had caused the suicide of his friend when the friend discovered the affair between Mastern and his wife. Mastern's acceptance of responsibility leads ultimately to his ostracism and death. Jack causes the death of Judge Irwin, who cannot acknowledge the action in his own past that had led to the suicide of the man he replaced in the American Electric Power Company. Irwin's suicide in the present sets in motion Jack's understanding of the past, the death of his old self and the emergence of a new one.

This pattern of not merely the interaction of present and past but of repetition echoes the trap of the Faulknerian historical consciousness. "Perhaps the only answer," Jack reminisces, "was that by the time we understood the pattern we are in, the definition we are making for ourselves, it is too late to break out of the box. . . . To break out of it, we must make a new self. But how . . . ? At least that was the way I argued it back then." And it is precisely Jack's change of heart which weans him from this bleak view. But Jack's conversion seems gratuitous; and neither it nor the novel's upbeat ending is quite convincing. Parricide, insight, and reversal are all present as in the Oedipal drama and its private modernist version, the psychoanalytic context. Yet what Jack "learns" is both too abstract and too sentimental. What he has done or desired does not have to be paid for; rather the lessons he carries away are the typical apolitical virtues of love and individual responsibility.

There is also a problem with the tone of Jack's narrative. In the "mackerel" passage quoted above, he lapses into a voice reminiscent of his earlier, cynical self. The flip use of "Dad" and the "mackerel" reference are too "in character" to suggest any new hard-won insight, and they undercut the seriousness of the passage rather than heightening its impact, as Warren had suggested the creative mixture of types of language would in his essay "Poetry—Pure and Impure." This failure of tonal control betrays, I think, the implausibility of Jack's rebirth into a new self.

There is another problem that demands resolution on both the personal and the political level—that of power and the relation of ends and means. Before Jack's conversion, and after he has talked with Willie about the problem of power, Jack meditates on the "theory of historical costs" and the way good intentions can lead to evil and vice versa. This is a view which Warren seems to have considerable sympathy for in later works such as *Brother to Dragons* and *Band of Angels*. Through Jack in *All the King's Men* Warren suggests the difficulties involved in judging past or present action and the necessity for a complexly ironic view of history.

The status of this view of history becomes problematic by the novel's conclusion. *All the King's Men* ends with the lone and scarred survivors, Jack and Anne Stanton, together; and Jack suggests that he will return eventually to politics to work for Hugh Miller. This evocation of Miller is bewildering, since he makes a brief appearance early in the novel as Willie's well-meaning but weak-kneed Attorney General who resigns because he can't stomach Stark's methods. If Jack (and Warren) accept the theory of historical costs, then it would seem that working for Miller is a repudiation of this philosophy of politics and power, a way of soothing one's conscience at the expense of political effectiveness. If Jack, however, repudiates the theory, then he would seem to work against the grain of Warren's own position. And this seems implausible since the novel ends on an upbeat note, notable more for its sonority than its clarity: "soon we shall go out of the house and out into the convulsion of the world, out of history into history and the awful responsibility of Time."

I must confess that I have no idea what these last lines mean. Warren does seem to want it both ways; and this, I think, makes up part of the contradiction that lies at the heart of the novel. Indeed, there is another contradiction of sorts at the end. Warren sets forth a view of freedom and responsibility that is gained through the costly confrontation with past and present reality. Jack Burden seems to have escaped the repetitious pattern of history. Yet Jack notes the irony of living in Irwin's house and writing about Cass Mastern. It is, he thinks, "a situation . . . too much like the world in which we live from birth to death, and the humor of it grows stale from repetition." This would suggest that Jack still suspects that he is caught in the process of time marked by repetition not freedom: entrapment not freedom is his fate. But his observation is followed immediately by the brave words of the ending.

I suspect that the confusion in *All the King's Men* has something to do with the fact that the relationship between the two stories—Willie's and Jack's—is never satisfactorily worked out. *All the King's Men* begins as a political story of a poor boy who rises to power, his attempts to break the "interests," and the personal, political, and moral costs involved. As seen through Jack's voice this would have made a fine and rather unique southern (and American) novel. Yet *All the King's Men* gradually becomes the story of Jack Burden's search for his father, i.e., the search for knowledge of his own past that will free him for the future. The two stories are only tenuously connected, and the linking device—Willie's desire to find incriminating information about Irwin—is not entirely convincing. By the end the Stark story has become a backdrop for Burden's quest and

Stark's death a way of precipitating a resolution of the quest. One might argue that the two stories mirror one another: Jack and Willie both do harm in the process of doing good. And both win through to insight, though Willie perishes. Yet the insight Jack attains is "only" personal and fails to illuminate the historical, ethical, and political issues raised by the Stark story. A political leader's use of bad means to achieve good ends is not finally in the same universe of moral discourse with the similar actions of an individual that have only circumscribed implications.

Thus what promised to be a profound political novel ends by being swallowed up by a private quest for identity, a form of secular salvation. In C. Vann Woodward's analysis of Tom Watson and the Populist movement, we can see some of the reasons for the failure of Watson and the Populist movement. But with *All the King's Men* it is difficult to discover what we are to learn from Willie Stark's story. It is less a matter of complexity or ambiguity here than that Warren seems to lose interest in the political issue altogether. Paradoxically, then, where Faulkner's *Absalom, Absalom!* and *Go Down, Moses* begin as private quests of apparently limited implication and end by engaging the "awful responsibility of Time" and the question of responsibility for one's individual and collective past, *All the King's Men* begins with the wider political world and ends by withdrawing from it into the rhetorical resolution of a private quest. Consciousness defeats action; the private vision, the public involvement; the ironic son, the strong fathers.

Chronology

1905   Born April 24 in Guthrie, Kentucky, to Robert Franklin Warren, a banker, and Anna Ruth Penn Warren, a schoolteacher.

1920   Accidentally blinded in one eye by stone thrown by his brother.

1921–25   Attends Vanderbilt University, where he studies poetry under John Crowe Ransom and Donald Davidson. Publishes poems in college magazines. Graduates *summa cum laude.*

1925–27   Does graduate work in English at the University of California, Berkeley, where he receives M.A.

1927–28   Does graduate work at Yale University.

1928–30   Attends Oxford on a Rhodes Scholarship. While there, publishes first book, *John Brown: The Making of a Martyr.* Receives B.Litt. from Oxford. Marries Emma Brescia.

1930–34   Begins academic profession—holds appointments at various southern universities. Publishes first fiction, and writes two novels which are rejected by publishers.

1935   *Thirty-Six Poems.* Founds journal *Southern Review* with Cleanth Brooks, Charles W. Pipkin, and Albert Erskine.

1936   Receives Houghton Mifflin Literary Fellowship Award. Edits first of many books with Cleanth Brooks, *An Approach to Literature* (also edited by John T. Purser).

1939   *Night Rider.* Travels to Italy on first Guggenheim Fellowship. Writes unpublished verse play, "Proud Flesh," whose hero is prototype of Willie Stark of *All the King's Men.*

1942   Becomes Professor of English at the University of Minnesota. *Eleven Poems on the Same Theme.*

1943   *At Heaven's Gate.*

1944   *Selected Poems: 1923–1943.*

1946   *All the King's Men,* which receives both the Pulitzer Prize and the National Book Award.

1947   *The Circus in the Attic, and Other Stories.*

1950   *World Enough and Time: A Romantic Novel.* Divorced from Emma Brescia.

1952   Marries author Eleanor Clark, by whom he has two children, Rosanna and Gabriel.

1953   *Brother to Dragons: A Tale in Verse and Voices.*

1955   *Band of Angels.* Father dies.

1956   *Segregation: The Inner Conflict in the South.*

1957   *Promises: Poems 1954–1956,* which receives both the Pulitzer Prize and the National Book Award, as well as the Edna St. Vincent Millay Prize of the Poetry Society of America.

1958   *Selected Essays.*

1959   *The Cave.*

1960   *You, Emperors and Others: Poems 1957–1960.*

1961   *Wilderness: A Tale of the Civil War* and *The Legacy of the Civil War: Meditations on the Centennial.* Appointed Professor of English at Yale University.

1964   *Flood: A Romance of Our Time.*

1966   *Selected Poems: New and Old 1923–1966,* which is awarded Bollingen Prize in poetry from Yale University.

1968   *Incarnations: Poems 1966–1968.*

1969   *Audubon: A Vision,* which receives both the Van Wyck Brooks Award and the National Medal for Literature in 1970.

1974   *Or Else: Poem/Poems 1968–1974.* Delivers third annual Jefferson Lecture in the Humanities for the National Endowment for the Humanities.

1975   Receives the Emerson-Thoreau Award of the American Academy of Arts and Sciences.

1977   *A Place to Come To.*

1978   *Now and Then: Poems 1976–1978,* which receives the Pulitzer Prize.

1979   Revision of *Brothers to Dragons: A Tale in Verse and Voices*.

1980   *Being Here: Poetry 1977–1980*. Awarded the Presidential Medal of Freedom.

1983   *Chief Joseph of the Nez Perce*.

1985   *New and Selected Poems: 1923–1985*.

1986   Appointed the first Poet Laureate of the United States.

Contributors

HAROLD BLOOM, Sterling Professor of the Humanities at Yale University, is the author of *The Anxiety of Influence, Poetry and Repression*, and many other volumes of literary criticism. His forthcoming study, *Freud: Transference and Authority*, attempts a full-scale reading of all of Freud's major writings. A MacArthur Prize Fellow, he is general editor of five series of literary criticism published by Chelsea House. During 1987–88, he was appointed Charles Eliot Norton Professor of Poetry at Harvard University.

CHARLES KAPLAN teaches at San Fernando Valley State College, Northridge, California. He is the author of *Literature in America: The Modern Age*.

JONATHAN BAUMBACH teaches in the English Department of Brooklyn College and is the author of *The Landscape of Nightmare* and several works of short fiction.

ARTHUR MIZENER, Professor Emeritus of English at Cornell University, is the author of biographical studies of F. Scott Fitzgerald and Ford Madox Ford.

ALLEN SHEPHERD is Professor of English at the University of Vermont.

MURRAY KRIEGER, Professor of English and Comparative Literature and Director of the Program in Literary Criticism at the University of California at Irvine, is the author of *The Tragic Vision* and *The Classic Vision*.

RICHARD GRAY teaches in the Department of Literature at the University of Essex, England. He is the author of *The Literature of Memory: Modern Writers of the American South*.

SIMONE VAUTHIER teaches in the English Department at the Université de Strasbourg.

RICHARD G. LAW, Associate Professor of English at Washington State University, has published articles on Robert Penn Warren in *American Literature, The Southern Literary Journal,* and *Studies in American Fiction.*

RICHARD H. KING teaches in the Department of Philosophy at the University of the District of Columbia. He is the author of *A Southern Renaissance: The Cultural Awakening of the American South, 1930–1955.*

Bibliography

Bauerle, Richard F. "The Emblematic Opening of Warren's *All the King's Men*." *Papers on Language and Literature* 8 (1972): 312–14.

Bohner, Charles H. *Robert Penn Warren*. New York: Twayne, 1964.

Booth, Wayne C. *The Rhetoric of Fiction*. Chicago: University of Chicago Press, 1961.

Bradbury, John M. *The Fugitives: A Critical Account*. Chapel Hill: University of North Carolina Press, 1957.

Carnegie Studies in English 3 (1957). A symposium on *All the King's Men*.

Casper, Leonard. *Robert Penn Warren: The Dark and Bloody Ground*. Westport, Conn.: Greenwood, 1960.

Chambers, Robert H., ed. *Twentieth Century Interpretations of* All the King's Men: *A Critical Handbook*. Belmont, Calif.: Wadsworth Publishing Co., 1976.

Grimshaw, James A., Jr. "Robert Penn Warren's *All the King's Men:* An Annotated Checklist of Criticism." *Resources of American Literary Study* 6 (1976): 23–69.

Guttenberg, Barnett. *Web of Being*. Nashville: Vanderbilt University Press, 1975.

Heilman, Robert B. "Melpomene as Wallflower; or, the Reading of Tragedy." In *Robert Penn Warren: A Collection of Critical Essays,* edited by John Lewis Longley, Jr., 82–95. New York: New York University Press, 1965.

Johnson, Glenn M. "The Pastness of *All the King's Men*." *American Literature* 50 (1980): 553–57.

Jones, Madison. "Robert Penn Warren as Novelist." In *A Southern Renascence Man: Views of Robert Penn Warren,* edited by Walter B. Edgar, 39–57. Baton Rouge: Louisiana State University Press, 1984.

Justus, James H. *The Achievement of Robert Penn Warren*. Baton Rouge: Louisiana State University Press, 1981.

———. "Warren and the Doctrine of Complicity." *Four Quartets* 21, no. 5 (1972): 93–99.

Katope, Christopher G. "Robert Penn Warren's *All the King's Men:* A Novel of 'Pure Imagination.' " *Texas Studies in Literature and Language* 12 (1970): 493–510.

Longley, John L., Jr. *Robert Penn Warren: A Collection of Critical Essays*. New York: New York University Press, 1965.

Mansfield, Luther Stearns. "History and the Historical Process in *All the King's Men*." *Centennial Review* 22 (1978): 214–30.

Meckier, Jerome. "Burden's Complaint: The Disintegrated Personality as Theme and Style in Robert Penn Warren's *All the King's Men*." *Studies in the Novel* 2, no. 1 (1970): 7–21.

161

Nakadate, Neil, ed. *Robert Penn Warren: Critical Perspectives*. Lexington: University of Kentucky Press, 1981.

Namba, Tatsuo. "Regionalism in Robert Penn Warren's *All the King's Men*." *Studies in American Literature* 8 (1972): 63–79.

Olson, David B. "Jack Burden and the Ending of *All the King's Men*." *Mississippi Quarterly* 26 (1973): 165–76.

Rubin, L. D., ed. *All the King's Meanings*. Baton Rouge: Louisiana State University Press, 1957.

Scouten, Arthur H. "Warren, Huey Long, and *All the King's Men*." *Four Quartets* 21, no. 4 (1972): 23–26.

Shepherd Allen. " 'Clean Hands and Pure Heart': Hugh Miller in Robert Penn Warren's *All the King's Men*." *Notes on Contemporary Literature* 11, no. 3 (1981): 3–5.

———. "Warren's *All the King's Men*: Using the Author's Guide to the Novel." *English Journal* 62 (1973): 704–8.

Slack, Robert C. "Willie Stark and William James." In *In Honor of Austen Wright*, edited by Joseph Baim, Ann L. Hayes, and Robert J. Gangewere, 71–79. Pittsburgh: Carnegie-Mellon University, 1972.

Snipes, Katherine. *Robert Penn Warren*. New York: Ungar, 1983.

Stanzel, Franz. *Narrative Situations in the Novel*. Bloomington: Indiana University Press, 1971.

Strout, Cushing. "*All the King's Men* and the Shadow of William James." *Southern Review* 6 (1970): 920–34.

Welch, Dennis M. "Image Making: Politics and Character Development in *All the King's Men*." *Hartford Studies in Literature* 8 (1976): 155–77.

Wilcox, Earl J. " 'A Cause for Laughter, A Thing for Tears': Humor in *All the King's Men*." *Southern Literary Journal* 12, no. 1 (1979): 27–35.

Winchell, Mark Royden. "O Happy Sin! *Felix Culpa* in *All the King's Men*." *Mississippi Quarterly* 31 (1978): 570–80.

Acknowledgments

"Jack Burden: Modern Ishmael" by Charles Kaplan from *College English* 22, no. 1 (October 1960), © 1960 by the National Council of Teachers of English. Reprinted by permission of the publishers.

"The Metaphysics of Demagoguery: *All the King's Men*" (originally entitled "The Metaphysics of Demagoguery: *All the King's Men* by Robert Penn Warren") by Jonathan Baumbach from *The Landscape of Nightmare: Studies in the Contemporary American Novel* by Jonathan Baumbach, © 1965 by New York University. Reprinted by permission of New York University Press.

"Robert Penn Warren: *All the King's Men*" by Arthur Mizener from *The Southern Review* 3 (1967), © 1967 by Arthur Mizener. Reprinted by permission.

"Robert Penn Warren as a Philosophical Novelist" by Allen Shepherd from *Western Humanities Review* 24, no. 2 (Spring 1970), © 1970 by the University of Utah. Reprinted by permission.

"The Assumption of the 'Burden' of History in *All the King's Men*" by Murray Krieger from *The Classic Vision: The Retreat from Extremity in Modern Literature* by Murray Krieger, © 1971 by the Johns Hopkins University Press, Baltimore/London. Reprinted by permission of the Johns Hopkins University Press.

"The American Novelist and American History: A Revaluation of *All the King's Men*" by Richard Gray from *Journal of American Studies* 6, no. 3 (December 1972), © 1972 by Cambridge University Press. Reprinted by permission.

"The Case of the Vanishing Narratee: An Inquiry into *All the King's Men*" by Simone Vauthier from *The Southern Literary Journal* 6, no. 2 (Spring 1974), © 1974 by the Department of English, University of North Carolina at Chapel Hill. Reprinted by permission of *The Southern Literary Journal*.

" 'The Case of the Upright Judge': The Nature of Truth in *All the King's Men*" by Richard G. Law from *Studies in American Fiction* 6, no. 1 (Spring 1978), © 1978 by Northeastern University. Reprinted by permission.

Index

165